The LORD'S TAVERNERS STICKY WICKET Book

The LORD'S TAVERNERS STICKY WICKET Book

**Edited by Tim Rice,
aided and abetted by
William Rushton**

QUEEN ANNE PRESS

MACDONALD AND JANE'S
LONDON AND SYDNEY

Acknowledgements

The publishers would like to thank the following for providing photographs:

BBC Photographs (page 119); Capital Press Photo Agency (page 142); Chris Capstick (page 111); Central Press Photos (page 49); Desmond O'Neill Features (page 50); Patrick Eagar (pages 19, 26, 37, 46, 74, 92, 124, 137, 144); Jeff Jones (pages 99, 111); Roger Kemp (pages 14, 29, 53, 70, 87, 122, 131, 147, 154); London Weekend Television (page 68); Jon Lyons (pages 105, 116); Press Association (pages 40, 96); Rex Features (pages 58, 78, 82, 111, 134, 140, 150); Syndication International (pages 126, 127); Pat Ward (page 90).

First published in 1979 by Queen Anne Press, Macdonald and Jane's Publishers Limited, Paulton House, 8 Shepherdess Walk, London N1 7LW

ISBN 0354 08559 X

Designed by Janet James
Jacket illustrations by William Rushton: the one on the front depicts a typical Taverners' team, the back the typical remains of a typical Taverners' team . . .

Typeset in Great Britain by Tradespools Limited, Frome, Somerset
Printed and bound in Great Britain by William Clowes & Sons Limited, Beccles, Suffolk

Contents

Illustrations by William Rushton and Bill Tidy

It is a bit difficult to be certain whether this book has been written by cricketing writers or writing cricketers. The problem is that public success is not always the same thing as personal satisfaction and I wouldn't be at all surprised if some of the successful writers would not rather be known for their cricket and vice versa. But whatever the case, all the contributors are agreed about one thing and that is their ambition to raise money to bring the opportunity to play cricket to more young people.

Raising money is not unlike batting on a sticky wicket and it says a lot for the batting skill of the Taverners that so far they have raised nearly £900,000 and I hope that with the publication of this book they will score with a full toss over the boundary.

Philip

JUST WHO ARE THE LORD'S TAVERNERS?

I shall give you a clue – Lord's. No, not a peer of the realm, but the cricket ground at St John's Wood. Tavern? Beer? Conviviality? Sport? Yes! You have it in one. So cricket and the friendliness which comes from sharing a pint together were the ingredients for the birth of the Lord's Taverners. This association has even been described as 'someone stirred a pint of beer with a cricket bat and up floated a Lord's Taverner'.

In 1950 a bunch of cricketing actors and acting cricketers used to assemble outside the famous Tavern at Lord's (now extinct but re-built). There, they would watch Compton and Edrich in their heyday weave their mastery in the sunshine. In those far off days, there was little television and so most of the actors waiting for the curtain to go up at 8.00pm, occupied the time by watching cricket until close of play at 6.30pm. A convenient arrangement, and one which gave birth to the Lord's Taverners.

This artistic group of cricket lovers decided to band together to put back into the game a few pounds for all the fun they had had, from both watching and playing the noblest of games.

Jack Payne, Bruce Seton, John Snagge and Martin Boddey were some of the earliest members. They were speedily joined by Sir John Mills, the first president, Sir Laurence Olivier, Sir Richard Attenborough, the Boulting brothers, and a host of other illustrious names. The first Ball was held at the Grosvenor House in July 1951, and attended by the Princess Elizabeth and HRH Prince Philip the Duke of Edinburgh. Prince Philip became Patron and 'Twelfth Man' of the Lord's Taverners, and has remained so for the past thirty years.

The whole thing was a gamble. The Lord's Taverners had no serious charitable objectives in the early days, and their humble annual offerings were presented to the National Playing Fields Association at the suggestion of our Patron. But like Topsy, the charity grew in both membership and success in fund-raising. By the time the Lord's Taverners celebrated their twenty-first birthday, they had put back £250,000 into youth cricket. Their achievements were celebrated at a banquet held at the Mansion House and attended by HRH Prince Philip.

Membership had now increased to six hundred, and included famous cricketers, businessmen prominent in their profession, as well as Prime Ministers and top politicians. By the time our Silver Jubilee arrived in 1975, the charity was 'having a go' at staging not only celebrity cricket matches but boxing, horse racing, golf, motor-racing and the famous BBC television show *It's a Knock-Out*. Social events included sell-out lunches at the Café Royal in the spring and at Christmas for seven hundred guests. The culmination of the year's activities was always the now famous President's Ball at the Grosvenor House Hotel, where twelve hundred supporters dance the night away for the charity.

These events and others continue today unabated. Over the past six years the Lord's Taverners have raised £100,000 per annum and in 1978 the charity were only £36 short of the total sum raised in the first twenty-one years! This is not said in any boastful manner, but illustrates the growth pattern which is now firmly established. So, from humble beginnings, we are very near to reaching our first million pounds! All credit to the founders way back in 1950, who had the courage and vision to start what has now turned into a success story.

Today, the charity gives away eighty-five pence in every pound, and supports sport for youth and in particular cricket; also adventure playgrounds through the National Playing Fields Association and, very important, for handicapped children mini-buses known as 'New Horizons'. A widening of our charitable objectives has broadened our national appeal with both members, sponsors and beneficiaries alike.

The Lord's Taverners now have one thousand additional supporters, known as Friends of the Lord's Taverners, whose numbers are on the increase. Regional cells have also been established all over the country to raise funds and have fun.

The key to our success story is our celebrities in the world of entertainment and sport. Their unstinting support for our charity has enabled us to ride the rough seas of inflation, which have affected many other charities. Without their contributions to our *Sticky Wicket Book*, it would not have been possible. It has been a great privilege to serve them as Director for the past eight years or so.

With the continuing support of a royal patron we are confident that we can play our small part in British society, which is justly proud of its charitable heritage.

Anthony Swainson, OBE
The Director

TEAM TALK

Welcome, my fellow Taverners, to these pages. May I, as your captain on this auspicious literary occasion, thank you one and all for your outbursts of creative activity. With the exception of Willie Rushton's reproduction of my features in cartoon form (see front cover) your contributions are beyond criticism. It hurts to be depicted as the thirteenth most handsome individual in a group of thirteen, all the more so when one of the number is an emu, but in the interests of team spirit I shall dwell no more upon this distressing topic. May I just refer readers to an early issue of *Cosmopolitan* (I think it was about May 1972) which I graced as Bachelor of the Month. There you will find a far more accurate portrayal of the Rice that my close friends know and love – it's a photograph too, not a mere drawing. There is also quite a good shot of me in the Icelandic *Jesus Christ Superstar* programme notes, taken shortly before we opened in Reykjavik. Who can forget the superb performance given by Gerd Nördstrom, or was it Nörd Gerdstrom . . . but I digress.

This is a team effort, and I am merely your humble leader. It has been a struggle extracting a finely-cut diamond from the glittering yet disparate *mélange* of talents available to me, but with the help of my fellow selectors (in particular Mr C.B. Howland, Captain J.A.R. Swainson and Ms Kirsty Ennever) I believe that the near-impossible has been achieved. But then I am used to captaining teams within whose deceptively peaceful ranks lurks potential chaos, through whose placid surface total bedlam continually threatens to burst. For some years now I have captained Heartaches CC, and I have seen it all.

Mike Brearley's problems are chickenfeed compared with mine. He knows that the eleven men selected to play in his team will turn up. Mrs Botham will not pull her old man out of the team at the last minute because the in-laws are coming to stay. Bob Taylor never takes his summer holiday in the summer. Graham Gooch's car will not break down on the way to the ground. David Gower does not go the The Oval when the match is being played at Edgbaston. Bob Willis does not leave halfway through the other side's innings because he has to appear on *Juke Box Jury*. Geoff Boycott brings his own flannels, and his own box. Mike Hendrick's dog does not follow him on to the pitch. All these are problems I have had to face in recent seasons, and if Brearers had just some of them on his plate, his record as England skipper would not be half as good as it is.

It is a miracle that Heartaches win any matches at all, but they do. It has to be dynamic leadership that has helped the lads in red, pink and green overcome these handicaps. It is that leadership I hope I have brought to you, fellow Taverners, and to this book.

I wish I had seen the front cover before the final proofs were passed though.

THE SELECTORS

Tim Rice (Captain and Editor)
Willie Rushton (Vice-Captain)

For the Taverners
Chris Howland (Chairman)
Anthony Swainson (Director)

For Queen Anne Press
Alan Smith (Publisher)
Kirsty Ennever (Editor's Editor)

The Team

PATRICK
MOORE
Night-Watchman

THE NIGHT-WATCHMAN

Cricket is a curious game. Generally speaking, one is not expected to do everything. There is no finer sight than Derek Randall in full cry, but I doubt whether he would ever expect to take eight or nine wickets in an innings against the Australians. As a fast bowler Bob Willis has no peer, but I think he would be slightly surprised to make a Test match century. And going back a few years, there have been some pretty bad fielders; I never saw 'Dainty' Ironmonger, but I gather that his catching ability was not markedly better than my own.

On the other hand, there are snags to this sort of attitude, and I have been acutely conscious of them over the years. When I began to play cricket, which was not until I was in my late teens, I realised at once that I had not one ounce of ability. I am no greyhound – someone once said that I gave every impression of having been somewhat hastily constructed, and I am not prepared to issue a denial – and I have no eye at all. I tried to bowl fast, with a total lack of success. I then tried swing, but the swing existed only in my imagination. Off-breaks were no better. Finally, I made the great decision, and started to bowl leg-spin at medium pace, off a long, bounding run which has been likened to a kangaroo performing a barn-dance. In my own realm, that of the village green, my new technique worked; and until 1977, when I had a rather nasty accident, I collected a crop of wickets each year. (I hope to do so again ere long.)

Please do not misunderstand me. I am no Wright or Hollies or Benaud, and if I were able to collect half a dozen wickets against, say, East Wittering, I would be completely satisfied. All the same, it paid dividends.

Batting? Well, my ambition has always been to score a hundred runs – not in a single innings, but in a season. I have never done so, and at the age of fifty-six I fear that the goal will forever elude me, though I continue to have my pipe-dreams. Last season, playing for my own club of Selsey, I amassed the grand total of four runs, two of which came from a snick through the slips in the penultimate match. This sounds quite in order; as a leg-breaker I am not expected to score runs, and the layman would well say 'Fair enough. Go in number eleven, and who cares?'.

Yet – and this is the point – things do not work out that way. Being a number eleven in a tight finish is no joke at all. More than once I have walked reluctantly to the wicket, knowing (a) that our best bat was 75 not out, (b) that we needed one run to tie and two to win, (c) that he was stranded at the non-striker's end, and (d) that I had to survive a complete over from a bowler whose pace seemed at that moment to be rather greater than Lindwall's. It is enough to make anyone's ganglions vibrate.

If you go in at number ten, all is well. The psychology is utterly different – if you are out first ball, there is still someone coming in after you to hold the fort. It is at number eleven that the real test of nerve comes.

Mind you, most number eleven batsmen can make at least some sort of a show. (Did not Rhodes once bat in that position for England?) They can also do the night-watchman's job, or, in the case of a village match, the tea-watchman's job. If

the vicar is next in, and dislikes the idea of facing a single over before the kettle boils and everything comes to a temporary halt, the job is often handed over to the usual number eleven – to play out 'just a few balls'. Once again, most number eleven bats can cope. I freely admit that I can't. I have two shots; one is a cow-swipe to leg, and the other is a desperate forward swat. I play these in strict rotation, and any bowler who knows me will at once send down a straight delivery which I am more or less certain to miss.

I recall one episode, years ago, when I was batting for a village (not Selsey) in the exalted position of number seven, because the regular number seven said that he had no wish to play himself in twice, and tea was due. I had to survive two overs. I managed one, aided by two dropped catches and an astounding degree of luck, but was out to the second ball of the last pre-tea over. Number seven, muttering darkly, came to take my place. You can guess the result. That cost me a round of drinks in the pub afterwards.

There is, mercifully, a lighter side, when there is a healthy score on the board and number eleven is allowed to 'have a crack' to see what happens. This is the moment when he really fancies his chances, though once again there are snags. In my young days I captained the Visitors against a team in the Channel Islands, and going in last I connected with two successive deliveries, both of which soared over square-leg, over the cliff, and into the sea. That was the end of the match; there were no more balls!

Just once in a lifetime comes that great moment when the number eleven makes a real score. That happened to me when I was in my twenties. Going in with the score at 27 for 9, I swung to leg and actually started to connect. Suddenly I was made aware that I was on 49. I couldn't believe it – was it possible that I would complete my half-century? The bowler bowled; I went to drive the ball back over his head; there was a curious snick, and I had hit a boundary – not over the bowler's head, but over the wicket-keeper's. My half-century was in the bag. The next ball was straight, and that was that. But I had had my hour of glory, even if I had been dropped about eight times (in the local newspaper report, it was said that I had had luck enough for two whole teams). Even the fact that I didn't make another run for the rest of the season failed to take the edge off my elation.

But seriously, what can the night-watchman do? When I go down to the local nets (as I do, very regularly), it is rather pointless for me to occupy the crease. The time available should be reserved for my betters. There are two ways of looking at any problem, of course, and I am forced to concede that I am an exceptional case. Most number elevens can learn to defend, at least . . . but it is essential to keep a sense of proportion. I am wearily resigned to knowing that if I am sent in as a tea-watchman, or if I am required to play a passive part in a last-wicket partnership, the result is virtually certain to be disastrous. Have sympathy for those such as me . . . please.

I will end, if I may, with a pathetic tale which takes me back only a few months – to the 1978 season. We batted first, and things went wrong from the start. Our best stroke-maker made an uncharacteristically elementary mistake of playing a fast delivery with his skull instead of the bat; our stonewaller swallowed a fly just as he was preparing to go forward, and sat on his wicket; our hitter was completely beaten by a ball which slipped from the bowler's hand, described a graceful parabola and landed on the middle stump. We scraped about thirty runs, which was not nearly enough, but at least we had one reliable player who looked well set. As I came in to face the last three balls of an over, he gave me an encouraging nod.

'Don't worry. Just stay there, and I'll keep you away from it. Leave it to me.'

I took guard. I was facing a slow off-spinner. Delivery number one came down; I blocked it. Number two was similar; I blocked it. A thought flashed through my mind.

'If I were that bowler, bowling against *me*', it went, 'I would now send down a fast, non-spinning yorker on the wicket. If he has the sense to do that, I have no answer.'

He did.

I hadn't.

R.I.P.!

JOHN
ARLOTT

Tail-Ender

CRICKET THROUGH THE DRINKING GLASS

A short-pitched ball lifting at a batsman's eyes; a fast, low, wide, slip catch; a batsman on the kill, murdering any ball even slightly off length or line – these do not permit the delayed response or flawed judgement of alcohol. Cricket and drinking do not mix; certainly not serious cricket and serious drinking. That is why English county dressing rooms are such temperate places. A pint of beer to give labouring fast bowlers something to sweat out (Arthur Carr always ordered one for Harold Larwood) is the only drink to be seen there during playing hours. Even at the end of play there are often almost as many glasses of fruit squash or milk as of shandy or beer; 'hard' liquor simply is not seen.

Away from the ground, matters may change, but little, except on occasions of celebration. It is different on tour, when Saturday night is party night; as it used to be in the domestic game before the advent of Sunday cricket. Even then beer was the general tipple; or occasionally wine – Hampshire and Glamorgan were partial to Beaujolais. The fact is that it is not possible to be a hard drinker and a first-class cricketer. One of the finest players of this century, a glorious athlete with a splendid physique, drank himself to sorry incompetence in less than ten years.

Yet there is a tradition of drink in the game –

'Then fill up your glass, he's the best that drinks most'

runs a line of the Reverend Regnell Cotton's eighteenth century poem which was adapted and adopted as the song of Hambledon, the first recorded great cricket club, whose spectators, members and players indulged their thirsts generously. We can assume that the players – professionals engaged to play for their backers' huge stakes – drank beer; for they came from the region of the anciently rich hop and barley fields and breweries of Farnham and Alton. An instruction of 1787, though, ordered:

'That every Player who does not appear on the Cricket Ground at twelve o'clock is to forfeit sixpence to be spent in Punch for the benefit of the other Players.'

John Nyren's *The Cricketers of My Time* is not only the most vivid study of cricketers, but contains a memorable passage about drink. On the spectators at Hambledon matches, he writes:

'How those fine brawn-faced fellows of farmers would drink to our success! And then, what stuff they had to drink! – Punch! – not your new *Ponche à la Romaine*, or *Ponche à la Groseille*, or your modern cat-lap milk punch – punch be-deviled; but good, unsophisticated John Bull stuff – stark! – that would stand on end – punch that would make a cat speak! Sixpence a bottle! We had not sixty millions of interest to pay in those days. The ale too! – not the modern horror under the same name, that drives as many men melancholy-mad as the hypocrites do; – not the beastliness of these days, that will make a fellow's inside like a shaking bog – and as rotten; but barleycorn, such as would put the souls of three butchers into one weaver. Ale that would flare like turpentine – genuine Boniface! – This immortal viand (for it was more than liquor) was vended as twopence per pint. The immeasurable villany of our vintners would, with their march of intellect (if ever they could get such a brewing), drive a pint of it out into a gallon.'

For the Hambledon members, matches – or meetings – were social, even bibulous occasions: one of the committee's first decisions was to build a wine cistern. An early club book records: 'A wet day, only three members present, nine bottles of wine.'

Richard Nyren, the captain, and William Barber, one of the players, in turn landlords of *The Bat and Ball Inn*, on Broadhalfpenny Down where the 'grand matches' were played, were responsible for the catering. They served dinner for a shilling a head; but were allowed sixpence a bottle corkage. A dinner for forty-nine members in 1791 came to £39.4s which allowed £36.15s for wine. Prices are indicated by the entry: 'The Stewards procure 3 Doz: of Madeira at 40s (the dozen, of course) from Mr Smith.'

The members themselves ordered the wine: and obviously took the matter seriously. 'Mr Richards be desired to send to Mr Gauntlett for a Hogshead of the best Port in bottle fit to drink immediately', runs one minute. An even more significant note is 'Ordered the wine to be returned to Messrs Gauntlett, not being approv'd'.

Madeira, sherry, port (by the pipe of 650 bottles), Carcavellos (a strong, sweet, dessert wine from Portugal) were ordered, but claret was the staple tipple. Of the annual subscription of three guineas, two were allocated for the cricket and dinners; and 'the overplus shall be laid out in claret to be drank on the Day of passing the Accompts'.

Members did not even need the excuse of cricket – 'Sept. 5th 1782: An extra Meeting to Eat Venison & drink Bonhams & Fitzherberts Claret'.

W.G. Grace, greatest of cricketers, was also a sturdy drinker. When Middlesex came to Bristol he used to greet their captain, A.J. Webbe, with 'She's down the well, Webbie, she's down the well'. 'She' meant 'The Widder' (widow) – Veuve Cliquot: a bottle of that champagne was hanging down the well to chill for dinner. During a long innings or a day in the field, 'The Old Man' used to fortify himself – in ample measure – with the unusual combination of Irish whisky, Angostura bitters and water.

His predilection for champagne was well known. Once, in 1889, he was playing for the South against the North at Scarborough. South were skittled out, and followed on on the third morning. Several of the North players were desperately anxious to catch the early train to Holbeck Feast; the alternative was a long, slow, late journey; and they believed, if they could get rid of W.G. cheaply, they would get away quickly. Three of them hit on the idea of presenting him with a bottle of champagne at lunchtime, in the hope that it would impair his eye. He accepted it with 'Thank'ee, Thank'ee' and, with his high-pitched laugh, 'Heh, heh, keep it cool, I'll drink it when I'm out'.

It is said that several times, as he hit one of the plotters for four, he chuckled 'I'll champagne yer'. Surely enough, W.G. batted for the rest of the day. His 154 saved the game – stumps were drawn when he was out – and the Yorkshiremen missed their train.

The greatest batsman of modern times, Sir Jack Hobbs, was strictly teetotal during his playing days – in fact his photograph was used on temperance posters. The drink

Percy Fender took out to him in a champagne glass when he equalled W.G. Grace's record number of 127 centuries was ginger ale. After he retired, though, he enjoyed hock or claret with his lunch or, better still, dinner. Best of all, he liked to telephone a friend from his shop in Fleet Street when he would open the conversation thus:

'Hullo, how are you?'

'Very well, thank you.'

'Could you feel a little better?'

'Well, perhaps.'

'Come on down to the shop then, we've got some bat oil down here.'

When his visitor arrived, Jack led him into Emil's – the old Wellington Restaurant, next door, long since gone – to share the half-bottle of champagne his nonconformist conscience would not allow him to drink alone. Sometimes, when the half was gone, he would say 'of course we shouldn't have another'. Then, eyes alight with mischief, and as if with inspiration, 'but Emil didn't have any; we'll open another so that he can have a glass' – and Emil always had it ready chilled, to produce upon his cue.

The last (alcoholic) drink Sir Jack ever had was champagne, just before he died, at Hove. His face was bright when he brought out the bottle: he sipped with happy anticipation, but already he was too frail to enjoy it.

'Put that gadget stopper in', he said. 'We'll finish it tomorrow', and then – 'Ah, that brings back memories'.

It still does.

LESLIE
THOMAS
Maidens

MY PARTNERSHIP WITH HUTTON

One of the least-known partnerships in the history of cricket was that of Sir Leonard Hutton and myself. It lasted throughout one season in the early 1960s and, while it could never have been expected to attain the fame and stature of Hutton and Washbrook, it was something I shall always treasure and remember.

At that time Sir Leonard had just retired from county cricket and I was a writer on the London *Evening News*, hacking away at anything that came along – including a weekly column on pop records (I forecast that The Beatles would flop in America!), coverage of the trial of Adolph Eichmann, a Royal tour in Australia, and the consecration of Coventry Cathedral. The newspaper engaged Sir Leonard to comment on a season's cricket when Pakistan were the tourists. To my intense delight I was given the task of writing articles from his experienced observations.

Our first assignment was at Worcester. On the damp, initial morning of the game I sat poised to record the words of this famous man. Unfortunately he didn't turn up till lunchtime. It was Tom Graveney's first season for Worcestershire, and here he was batting on that most idyllic of grounds, against unknown opposition, at the birth of a new season. I struggled to think what Hutton would have thought, wrote a few paragraphs, and was then intensely relieved to see the famous man himself, draped in a long black overcoat, standing some distance away gazing out over the green ground with the remote elegance of an ancient seer. I left my seat in the press box and hurried over to introduce myself and to show him his thoughts, as constructed by me.

He is a man of distinguished bearing, with a noble nose and china blue eyes. 'Aye', he said eventually, when he had read my efforts. 'That's just what I would have said. Come and have some lunch.'

That day he paid for lunch, and the next day I paid, and on the third day he brought sandwiches and I had a bag of crisps. On the following Monday my first television play was being screened by the BBC, and I spent the Worcestershire lunch hour writing an objective appraisal of it for my own newspaper. I had no time for lunch. The crisps would have to suffice until I got home that evening. Sir Leonard, having disposed of his sandwiches, now eyed the crisps and mentioned – as if in passing – that he was fond of such delicacies. I suggested he might like to help himself. He opened the packet and pinched out a handful, which he ate.

'Mind you', he said, having tasted them, 'they're better with salt.'

He then discovered the blue packet of salt, and having liberally sprinkled it into the packet he helped himself to another sample. This he apparently enjoyed so much that he took a third. When my turn came there were a few lonely crisps left curled in the bottom of the packet. Huffily, I said:

'You might as well finish them now.'

'Oh, no, lad', he said kindly. 'You finish them. After all they're *your* crisps.'

Sir Leonard had the quietest sense of humour I've ever known in anybody. But it was there. He could be deadly serious about the most outlandish matter and it wasn't until a faint, different light appeared in those singular eyes that it was apparent he was joking.

On one occasion during our season together he was in the bar at Trent Bridge, describing to a circle of current England players how Ernie Toshack, the great Australian bowler of the immediate post-war years, persisted in bowling at his legs in a Test match.

'Every ball was right there, on my legs', he said, while they listened and watched seriously. 'So I moved over to leg a bit . . . '

He demonstrated, shuffling a few inches to the left. The audience took it all in.

'And he still bowled at my legs, so I moved over a bit more . . . '

Everyone watched while he inched over a little further. The monologue and the action was repeated once more until Sir Leonard said:

'There was I batting over here and him still bowling on my legs – and there were the stumps left way over there.' It wasn't until then that we realised we were listening to a Yorkshire yarn.

Our partnership, I am pleased to recall, prospered. He once left me waiting in my car in the street while (he said) he went to help an old lady to cross the road. He told me that if only I could have been better at cricket, I had the right temperament and philosophy to be the ideal tourist in Australia. That is a compliment I did not take lightly.

As we travelled together through the county grounds of England, he frequently met with compliments himself. On many occasions a spectator would approach and say: 'Len', or 'Mister Hutton', or occasionally 'Sir Leonard', and would ask to shake him by the hand, 'because you've given me so much pleasure – just watching you bat'. I felt that was the greatest compliment anyone could pay a great cricketer.

We have not met for many years, although on occasions he has telephoned to discuss the Stock Exchange (of which I know nothing). His memory is still fresh with me, that of a great cricketer and a unique man.

At Edgbaston that year he was sitting in the press box and, despite being under contract to my own newspaper, was approached by a young and hopeful reporter from Birmingham.

'Sir Leonard', said this tyro cautiously, 'what do you think they're trying to do?'

Sir Leonard took the question in. Then he turned his eyes on the play for several minutes. A spin bowler was bowling to a defiant batsman.

'I think', said the great man, as the lad fumbled with his pencil and notebook, 'I think they're trying to get him out'.

RICHIE
BENAUD
Leg Spinner

A LOOSE FIXTURE

Unpaid debts abound in cricket: not the furtive ones involving grubby cash, but the important debts covering one's introduction to the more subtle mysteries of the sport.

I, for example, will never cease to be grateful to Frank Russell for his part in starting me off in London club and village cricket. 'The Parasites' hadn't been going all that long in 1960, and I was pressed into service for a match at Hampstead. Ian Craig was included in the side.

A warm ale and a deck chair later, I watched the bearded opposition fast bowler rush up and let fly with the opening delivery that had more of the virtues of pace than accuracy. It struck first slip a sickening blow in what, in cricketing terms, has always been known laughingly as 'the groin'.

There is no logical explanation for the fact that, when this happens, everyone at the ground, other than the victim, roars with laughter. Even so, it was a slightly daunting experience to begin one's higher cricket life in such a way. These days, of course, first slip would be fully kitted out – not only with groin protector, but with helmet and shin pads as well. We have come a long way in the past twenty years!

I have been mildly interested in club and village cricket since then, even breaking out of retirement five years ago to turn out for Ripe and Chalvington, a Sussex village team. Two of our friends, 'Chic' and 'Sparrow', are the Italian-cum-English and Welsh backbone of the team. The skipper is 'Jumping Joe', much experienced in the vagaries of village cricket over the past fifty years. It had taken three years planning to find a date on their carefully compiled fixture list when I was free of BBC television and other work commitments . . . but finally we settled on a Sunday in June.

It was very much a social affair. White burgundy and delicious ham, salmon and chicken sandwiches, in a second class carriage, set the scene for pertinent entries in Sparrow's diary. There were constant exhortations from the two team leaders that the opponents, Rottingdean, must be beaten on this occasion. There had been a spot of trouble with the umpiring last year apparently, not all that uncommon in cricket as well as other sport these days.

There was another minor sporting fixture being played the same day, the World Cup soccer match between East Germany and Holland, but that was unlikely to have any severe effect on the attendance at our event.

Hospitality on arrival at Old Mill House was superb, so too the ground which had been meticulously planned a couple of centuries ago with its entrance alongside the *Yew Tree* pub. Rumour had it that the beautifully spacious barns had seen much activity between cricketers and wenches in the eighteen-hundreds.

An hour later there was disquiet in the group. We were here, but where were they? Rottingdean so far hadn't appeared: not a player or a supporter. Was it too wet? Had they perhaps got wind of the grey-haired import from Australia?

Ninety minutes after the listed starting time, a 'phone call was made and our messenger returned, set-faced and asking to see the fixture list.

The home team compiler produced it and pointed firmly to the entry: Ripe and Chalvington v Rottingdean.

'You see', he said triumphantly, 'it's on our fixture list'.

'Ah', said the stuttering Sparrow. 'Quite s . . so.' 'B . b . b . but is it on theirs?'

Of course it wasn't. Rottingdean were playing another fixture thirty miles away.

It was a marvellous World Cup match to watch on television! I've not played since that day, preferring to stay in retirement, on the basis that someone up there may have been trying to save me from a fate worse than torn back muscles.

Looking around the world cricket scene at the moment, it's not too hard to see why an ageing leg spinner might decide to call it quits after a disaster of this kind. Leg spin bowling has disappeared from the game in England. Robin Hobbs was the last of the craft in first-class cricket, and has now come back as captain of Glamorgan. It is something of a transition from leg spinner to skipper, and a big sacrifice to make just for a game of cricket, but it's nice to see him back.

In the West Indies team, the only time we see over-the-wrist spin is when Roy Fredericks is pressed into commission, and even the stocky little left-hander declined the lure of the World Cup in 1979.

Australia have plenty of over-the-wrist spin in Sheffield Shield cricket, but in the Test side in recent times it has been of variable quantity and quality.

New Zealand don't bother at all, and it is left to the sub-continent teams, Pakistan and India, to carry on the Empire tradition started so long ago. No leg spinner showed his face for the limited-overs fixtures of 1979, the Prudential World Cup.

If I confess to a certain amount of frustration at this, then I hope it will be understood that I am simply biased in favour of the over-the-wrist bowler. Perhaps that bias blinds me to the logic of playing only fast and medium bowlers in limited-overs fixtures. Is it impossible for a leg spin bowler to be of any use in these matches?

In years past, there were many occasions in Sheffield Shield, Test matches and games for the touring side against counties where, in a race against the clock or against remaining overs, I was able to play a part in victory or in avoiding defeat. Has the game changed so much in fifteen years that this would no longer be possible? Are the batsmen of today so adept at hitting for four or six the leg break landing on a length and turning the width of the bat, that there would be no place for me?

Or, is it the same kind of modern thinking that has it that Bradman might have made as many runs these days, but they would have taken him three times as long against pedestrian medium pace?

What place I wonder would O'Reilly have had in limited-overs cricket in 1980. Would his team manager be saying 'Tiger . . . you'll have to change your style, or it's down to the second team at Ripe and Chalvington'.

I'd like to be there to hear him say it, and to hear the great man's reply – particularly if the match wasn't on the fixture list!

TIM
BROOKE-TAYLOR

Chinaman

LONG DISTANCE BOWLING

Having bowled with the longest run up ever at Lord's, I feel I am probably the world's greatest exponent, in fact the world's only exponent, of long distance bowling. (SEE PLAN)

The purpose of long distance bowling is to make an ageing, talentless bowler not unlike myself appear to be youthful and possibly even ('If only he'd taken it seriously') a bit useful. The art has been perfected after many years of playing for the Lord's Taverners.

Quite simply I cannot and do not want to bowl ever again in my life. Unlike my fellow team-mates, who try to conceal their disappointment when they are not asked to bowl, I try to conceal myself in case I am. Usually I can be found lurking behind an umpire, or if absolutely necessary a sight-screen. Sooner or later, though, that sickeningly hard ball is going to be lobbed over in my direction with the cheerful cry of 'Care to turn your arm over, Tim?'. My brain is screaming 'No. No. I'd sooner turn my ankle over', and yet for some extraordinary reason my mouth is saying 'Certainly Trevor, love to'. Love to?!! Trevor?!!

Well the first bit is quite easy (Fig 1). I start with a mark out of what appears to be a short run; but with several false stops and a lot of walking I eventually end up behind the sight-screens. So far so good; a few chuckles from the crowd and not a single muscle pulled.

First problem (Fig 2) there is usually a large dog behind – and using – the sight-screen. This monster has been trained from birth to dig his enormous teeth into any passing ball and 'retrieve'. To be fair, he cannot really be blamed, but you are not fair if a ton of dog flesh hurls itself at you with the intention of removing the ball from your hand or, if necessary, the ball and the hand.

The dog is firmly leashed, but I do not know this – so, like a cherry stone squeezed between two fingers, I shoot from behind the screens. This means a rather quicker start to my run up than I originally intended. In fact if a long run is to make any sense at all then this suicidal, heart-thumping pace will actually have to be increased.

(Fig 3) 'Why don't I just ease off a little? No it won't look right. But it's only for charity. Yes.'

(Fig 4) Pride makes me go a little bit faster. My chest is about to snap open. Will I never learn?

(Fig 5) Oh dear I've come to the funny circle part which doubles the length of the run. Never mind, this bit always gets a laugh.

(Fig 6) Not always.

(Fig 7) I try to think of other things to take my mind off the pain. How many births in the world would there be during my run up I wonder? How many deaths?

(Fig 8) Death is now my sole preoccupation. Surely the point of this function is to help people in distress, not to add to their numbers?

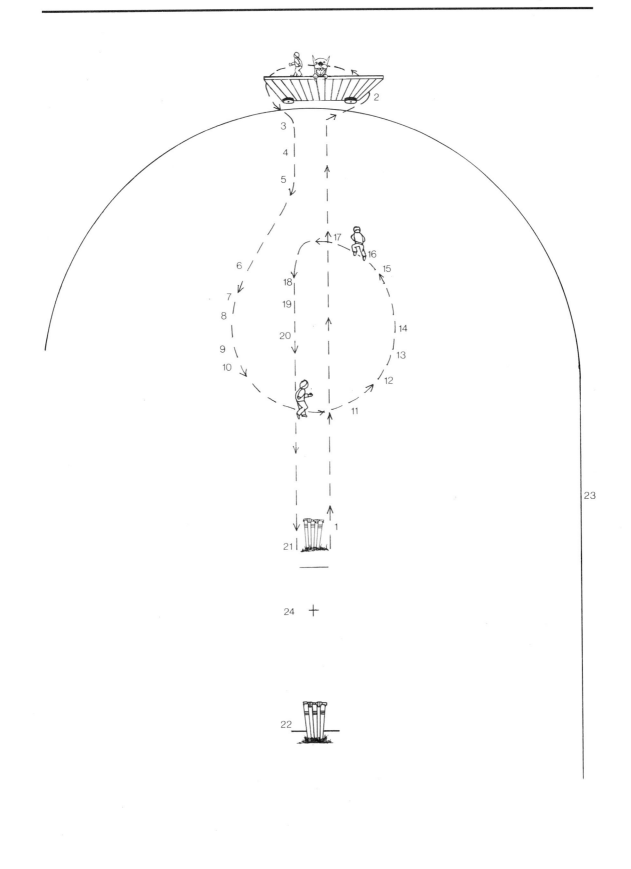

(Fig 9) Life insurance?

(Fig 10) Burial or cremation?

(Fig 11) What did happen to Lord Lucan?

(Fig 12) Never mind, worse things happen at sea. (Name one.)

(Fig 13) I must not think about poached haddock and trifle.

(Fig 14) Now all I can think about is poached haddock and trifle, and death, and where my kidney donor card is.

(Fig 15) 'The Two Goodies'?

(Fig 16) I wonder if it's raining in Walsall?

(Fig 17) To hell with Walsall, I'm dying here.

(Figs 18, 19 & 20) The brain has closed down.

(Fig 21) Umpire calls 'no ball'.

(Fig 22) Batsman hits a six.

(Fig 23) The crowd, who have been watching Racquel Welch arrive by parachute, turn back to watch the game.

(Fig 24) Five more balls to go. I tell a lie – SIX.

YOU CAN STICK IT
CRICKET.

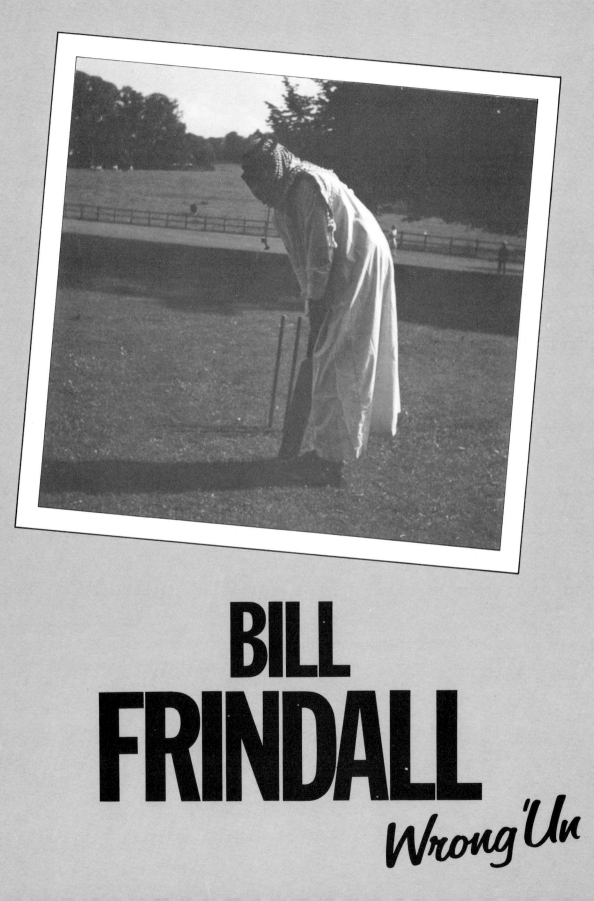

BILL
FRINDALL
Wrong 'Un

SCORING IN ARABIC

It all began at a party in Hampstead a few evenings before the Fifth Test between England and Australia at The Oval in August 1977. I was introduced to an Arab called Sheikh Aziz who promptly asked me which part of Abu Dhabi I came from. Before I could answer this somewhat unexpected enquiry (I was born in Epsom of Caucasian parents), Henry Blofield's girlfriend interrupted by assuring me that I could pass as an Arab.

She quickly bet me that I wouldn't score at the Test match dressed as an Arab. The bets soon mounted up and I felt compelled to take them on. I wanted to give the money to the Primary Club (the cricketers' charity which raises several thousand pounds each year for the Dorton House School for Blind Children), but the treasurer of Cancer Research was present and swiftly claimed the spoils of my promised ordeal.

The following is an unexpurgated transcript of a snatch of commentary from The Oval on the third morning of the Fifth Test. It was repeated on BBC radio's *Pick of the Week* and only the hysterics have been edited out.

Characters in order of appearances:
FS: Frederick Sewards Trueman
BJ: Brian Johnston
Arab: Bearded Wonder
FS: 'Who's that sat at the side of you, Johnners? Have you ever seen anything like that in your life?'
BJ: 'No, listeners would be rather amazed if they were to look in the box today – they might be amazed any day! On my right at the moment is a gentleman in Arab dress; it looks like an old sheet that he's got on.'
Arab: 'It's a dishdash.'
FS: 'It's a dish-wash!'
BJ: 'Anyway, we'll explain about it in a minute, as Thomson comes in now to bowl to Willis. In he comes, bowling from the Vauxhall End, and Willis goes to turn this on the leg side, misses it, and Marsh moves across. Now, what is your head-dress called – your Arab head-dress?'
Arab: 'I've got no idea. It was given to the gentleman I borrowed it from by King Hussein.'
BJ: 'He was sitting in the box and all of us came in and sort of pointed at him. One or two said: "Good morning" – like that (*at this point BJ unwisely attempted an Eastern accent*) – and he sort of muttered underneath his beard. And it is, in fact, done for a very good purpose, isn't it?'
Arab: 'Yes, I've been sponsored to the tune of something like £62 for Cancer Research.'
BJ: 'What, so long as you . . .'
Arab: 'I've got to stay all day, scoring, throughout the six hours of play, and . . .'
BJ: 'In your Arab dress?'
Arab: 'That's right.'
BJ: 'Careful we don't remove it from you!'
Arab: 'Careful!'

BJ: 'Now Thomson's coming in to bowl to Willis – and that one's another class stroke from Willis, this time through the covers. Two runs there, as Hughes chases it down towards the gasholder. That one he played between cover and extra cover. And we're seeing some good strokes from these numbers ten and eleven. So there's some good stuff. It's double figures for Willis – he goes on to 11: 191 for 9, and still 5 to Hendrick.'

FS: 'I hope Bill doesn't come to our house dressed like that because my sheepdog William will attack him. He'll think it's a mate!'

BJ: 'My terrier Minnie would have a go at him too!'

FS: 'No wonder King Hussein gave it away. Look at it!'

Arab: 'You're only jealous.'

FS: 'Jealous!'

BJ: 'And in comes Thomson now, to bowl to Willis. He bowls this one outside the leg stump – and he's glided that one for four. A lovely stroke there; any batsman would have been proud of that. It came down here at a rate of knots. No question of anybody stopping it from long-leg; Malone was down there but he couldn't get to it. So, a beautiful leg glide by Willis takes him to 15. England 195 for 9.'

Arab: 'A partnership of 21 – the third highest of the innings.'

BJ: 'The highest being 86, I can reveal to you, and the next one being 39 between Roope and Underwood; 86 was for the first wicket by Brearley and Boycott.'

FS: 'Reminds me of a story, seeing Frindall dressed like that.'

BJ: 'Is it repeatable on the air?'

FS: 'Oh, yes. It's about the fastest thing on two wheels in London – an Arab crossing Golders Green on a pushbike!'

LUNCH INTERVAL

In assigning the 'Lunch Interval' of *The Lord's Taverners Sticky Wicket Book* to me, which seems very appropriate, the Editor suggested that I might concoct a spoof menu. I gave this serious thought, but found it too restrictive. To have begun with some ploy about Grace would have been too obvious. To have associated any cricketer with duck in any of its forms would have been invidious. There are no dishes in the Western world using bats as an ingredient (not even the blood-sucking umpire bats). Hammond eggs would have dated me, and anyway I am allergic to puns.

I must confess, however, that had I ever sold ice-cream, which contrary to popular legend I never did, it would have given me great joy to have invented a speciality called *Coupe Jack Hobbs*.

I know that dates me too, but there was a cricketer indeed! He was the stroke player *par excellence*, who really was beautiful to watch. Hobbs and Sutcliffe opening for England! Sticky wickets never seemed to bother them. Nor did they feel it necessary to dress up like all-American footballers to face fast bowling. Were there really giants in those days when, in retrospect, the sun always seemed to shine in the summer and rain rarely stopped play?

I find it interesting that in recalling my interest in cricket over many years it is not the games I remember, which side won and which side lost, but the individual performances. Is this something to do with my nature as a dedicated (some might say rabid) individualist? Or is it something to do with the nature of the game? A cricket pitch is like a stage – set with stars expected to perform magnificently. So perhaps it is an intrinsic part of the nature of cricket that it is the great performances with bat and ball, and occasionally in the field, which are remembered.

Cricket is also peculiar in that despite being a big team game, the batsmen leave the field individually, taking their bow for success or hanging their heads after failure, in a way reminiscent of an opera house. (It is just as well that the Italians don't play cricket. In the tradition of La Scala, Milan, the century-makers might get flowers and cheers but the duck-makers would get catcalls and carrots.) It is this fact, that a cricket pitch is like a stage-set, which makes it such an ideal sport to watch on television. I must confess that, while I have been a member of the MCC for some fifteen years, most of my watching is now done 'on the box'.

There is, of course, something special about being present in person at any great sporting event – a Test match, the football Cup Final, Wimbledon, a world title boxing match ('the roar of the grease-paint, the smell of the crowd' as they say) but, while it may be bad for gate money, cricket is tailor-made for television.

In a football stadium the action can take place on any part of the field, but with cricket ninety per cent of what is happening is out on that distant twenty-two yard strip in the middle. There is no way, short of running on to the pitch – which never happened in more civilised times – that you can get there.

The electronic wonders of television like the zoom lens and, above all, the action replay, enable the spectator to see far more of the finer points in close up. You can see what the bowler is hoping to do with the ball and, on rare occasions, actually see it swing and move in the air.

Among the many things about cricket which I do not understand, the way a sudden change in the atmosphere can make the ball curve in the air is the most mysterious. It is not all that long ago that scientists were arguing that it was not possible for a bowler or a baseball pitcher to make the ball curve in the air – but high-speed photographs taken in wind-tunnels proved that they can. I am told that it is due to something called the Magnus Effect. I have never experienced this myself, though there have been times, when I was younger, when I have seen the whole world spin due to what might be called the Magnum Effect!

I would like to see the scientist taking a greater academic interest in cricket, with perhaps a university chair here and there, and PhDs in cricketology. These elevated people should certainly investigate that elusive entity called 'form', which applies to every sport. Expertise in all ball games must centre on co-ordination between hand and eye, and form must be connected with that co-ordination. So why can co-ordination be brilliant one day, and dreadful the next? Of one thing I am certain – it has little to do with fitness.

The sport at which I spend most time is game shooting. Sometimes I wake on a Saturday morning feeling so marvellous that I am convinced I am going to shoot brilliantly. Yet I may fail miserably. On other days, when I awake feeling bleary and perhaps even unwell with a slight cold, I go out reluctantly and, as a friend of mine puts it, 'shoot like a tiger'.

Curiously, the only scientific research into form of which I have heard – carried out on men shooting clay pigeons – suggested that they put up a better performance when they were slightly hung over!

I am also convinced that form is not just a matter of concentration. Excessive concentration can be death to good shooting, because one needs to be relaxed. I suspect that the same must be true of cricket and that excessive concentration may be the cause of many Test match failures among batsmen.

There may be a connection here with something else which my scientific friends have told me. It is commonly believed that the successful batsman keeps his eye on the ball until the last moment and then puts his bat to it. This cannot be true, at any rate with fast bowling. Larwood was timed as delivering a ball at more than ninety miles an hour. As it only has twenty yards to travel to the bat, the batsman has only about half a second to see the ball at all. His reaction time in getting his bat into position is so slow (however fast he thinks he is) that all he can do is to predict where the ball will be when he wants to hit it and put his bat there. It is this power to predict which makes for a good batsman, my scientific friends tell me.

Happily in shooting one has a little more time, though a grouse coming at you in a gale will not be much slower than the fast cricket ball.

The more I think about the problems of cricket and shooting the more comparable they seem. Like no two balls, no two birds are the same. They come at different angles and different speeds. Timing is everything and even the place where one is standing – footwork being everything – can often be stickier than any wicket.

There is a further point of similarity. Every sport should, on occasion, provide humbling experiences, which are so good for the soul. With the duck and the dropped dolly catch, cricket provides them in plenty. Shooting seems to provide them all the time. It is the 'easy' bird which seems to be sitting on the end of the barrel which is so often missed. And, of course, everybody sees it.

There can even be similarities in the score. On one rather good shoot, for example, a guest who was sadly off form when performing there for the first time had shot only four birds after firing fifty-four cartridges at the end of a rather hot drive. On looking down at the empty cases, his loader scratched his head and remarked '54 for 4. Sounds more like a cricket score!'

There is one way in which cricket has the edge over shooting and that is in connection with what is called empathy – the unconscious identification of oneself with the performer. The story of the bishop who mentally bowled googlies every time he walked down his cathedral aisle, wondering whether it might take spin, is no exaggeration. There is something about a beautifully timed cut or a great swipe to leg which, from our school days, we can all remember and almost feel when watching somebody else do it. This is something which women who have never played cricket can't quite understand. I feel sorry for them. They also miss the wonderfully nostalgic smell of mown grass and linseed oil, of which we used to use gallons on our bats. (Incidentally, do girls oil hockey sticks?)

To return to the theme of the Lunch Interval in concluding this 'dissertation' – which is what the Editor finally settled for – I could mention, not too immodestly I hope in view of my profession, that on my shoot the lunch is commonly regarded as 'the most reliable drive of the day'. This could, of course, be a barbed compliment suggesting that the pheasant drives are not so hot. But I think not.

If my shoot lunches are memorable, I hope it is partly because of the food and wine, but they are also an occasion for banter and good fellowship. International matches must be serious affairs, but for those millions of us who indulge in sport – as well as watch it – whether it be a fun shoot or a game on the village pitch, laughter and the love of friends are the prime attractions.

ROY
CASTLE
Long Leg

LONG LEG

I was rather alarmed at being asked to write from the above position as I have a distinct and lasting aversion to one of the words . . . *leg* I can put up with, even in the plural, but the *other* one! AAACH! It all happened a lo . . quite a while ago. I was included in a team to represent the Lord's Taverners against an Olde Englande Eleven at Lord's. It was a fund raising event in aid of our patron and Twelfth Man's worthy charity.

I was delighted to be playing on '*theee*' cricket table. All my boyhood imaginings were about to be realised and stories for my grandchildren were about to be born.

A beautiful day helped us all to draw a large crowd and, as usual, we 'personalities' fielded first. I was asked to field at lo . . er – rather extended leg: an unenviable position as you are always obstructing someone's view. The ploy here is to keep moving crab-like around the boundary until you bump into . . . er . . . rather extended *off*. Then you do the same thing in reverse, bobbing down for each delivery. That way you make no enemies in the crowd, but your captain begins to have his doubts – not to mention the – er – rather extended off! (The only cricketer to get the yellow card!)

However, this is not the reason for my aversion to *that* word. Olde Englande finished their innings, and had scored the usual two hundred odd runs – leaving us Lord's Taverners to get the winner in a moonlight scramble.

Some of our better players went in to bat first – your Barringtons in beards, your Cowdreys in glassless spectacles, and other such heavy disguises. We were well ahead of the clock. I was in the dressing room, watching all this on our telly, and working out a couple of comedy bits with Norman Wisdom (who had changed his name to *Wisden* for the day). We were both well aware that we hadn't been asked along to demonstrate our cricketing skills – not in the company of your Huttons, Washbrooks, Evans, Bedsers times identical two, and Edriches recurring. I remembered a little piece of acrobatics which was a surefire laugh without the necessity for props such as ladies' clothes, bicycles – or for that matter, apples instead of cricket balls. Norman and I rehearsed our parts gently, and felt quite confident.

'YOU'RE IN!'

I waddled out of the dressing room in borrowed pads and gloves, and found I had to walk through the famous and extremely unnerving Lo . . – er – rather extended room. I shuffled nervously past the blazers, badges, ties, pink gins, double chins, dripping moustaches and piercing stares. Eyes followed me but faces didn't. One man gave me a centimeter of a smile – he was a guest. The thought of facing Alec Bedser was a relief.

Suddenly my eyes reacted against the light and I was on my way to the wicket. This was it! I got my first laugh as I did my usual trip-up in the region of deep mid-off. More giggles as I took guard as a left-hander then proceeded to bat right-handed. I was nursed to 15 runs by Bedser and Co, at which stage Pete Murray, after a fine innings, was caught on the boundary. Without his trousers.

Next man in? Norman! He allowed himself only one luxury – his famous slanted cap. His much copied walk to the wicket gave the doubled up audience a taste of, and an appetite for, things to come. There was more clowning and even some more laughs. I took up the challenge and skied a big one to square leg, ran after it, and – just as one of the Edrich family was about to catch the ball – nudged it over the boundary with the highly held toe end of my bat. We were going well, entertainment wise anyway.

Now Norman and I were ready for our *pièce de resistance*! I nudged a ball to third man and we were off. As rehearsed, we transferred our bats into our respective right hands, crooked up our left arms and ran at each other as fast as we could go. We linked arms at full speed and held on. We spun high in the air like a bodyless helicopter. We reached the climax of our upward surge and began re-entry – without parachutes. Our thirteen-point landing received a gratifyingly huge laugh – well worth the laundry bill.

Finally I was out for 22 runs, and got a dream reception all the way back to the pavilion. I felt really good – and my performance had been on telly too! With cheers, whistles, and applause still ringing in my ears, I entered the – er – rather extended room. This was where my nightmare began. The contrast was like diving underwater from the side of a noisy indoor pool – driving suddenly through an underpass having had the car radio at full blast – jumping out of the frying pan into the fridge!

My eyes opened wide as I looked inside the room. There was a vibrating hush: a row of reddening faces, quivering moustaches, eyes like rear fog lights on a clear night. I still hadn't taken a step over the threshold – but there was no other way. I tried to walk nonchalantly, but I was like a gnat that had just landed on drying paint. My cricket boots became those of a deep sea diver, my imaginary braces were caught on an imaginary hook, I was walking against a conveyor belt. I desperately wanted to get through before the heat melted my contact lenses, before there were thirty-five coronaries in ten seconds. I swear the only faint glimmer of a smile was that on a photograph of the great W.G.

Three days later . . .

I was groping my way past the last gorgon, whose whisky was actually boiling in his hand, when I was aware of a rumbling which eventually seemed to form words. The teeth never parted company, but the message was forced through.

''Ampstead 'Eath's the place for that kind of stuff!'

I went over the wall. At last I was through! The assault course was over. I was still alive: just. The back patting resumed, autograph books were thrust under my nose, beer spilt over my arms and pads. I chanced a glance back into the . . . rather extended room. The occupants were quietly continuing the gnashing of teeth: doubtless awaiting the arrival of the unwitting Norman!

If I am ever asked to play at Lord's again, I shall demand two things:
1. To be allowed to field at '*short*' anywhere.
2. To have access to a private stage door to the dressing room.

So long! Long? AAACH!!

ERNIE WISE

Short Fine Leg

I LOVE CRICKET

As a Yorkshireman it's natural that I should be interested in cricket. I play an active part, too, and have played for the Lord's Taverners, of which Eric is currently president.

In my early years – well, that was only ten years ago – I decided that with my short, fat, hairy legs I had no choice but to opt for cricket. So many of the great players like Len Hutton, Jack Hobbs and Wilfred Rhodes were my schoolboy heroes, but I suppose, like so many cricket fans, to me the greatest cricketer of them all must be the legendary W.G. Grace.

Do you know that his cricketing career began in 1863 when he was only fifteen years of age? And that he continued playing until 1906, when he was fifty-eight! He scored 217 centuries, 126 of them in first-class cricket, and although his flailing bat won him immortality, he was a splendid bowler too and took over 2,800 wickets during his magnificent career.

Apart from his cricket, W.G. was a splendid runner and during the winter months he used to play association football, and also to hunt. And apart from all this, he still carried on a doctor's practice in Bristol.

I bet you are thinking: 'What an encyclopaedic knowledge little Ern has.' You are right, of course, but I'm also using up a lot of words to fill the editor's requirements. Honestly, the things I do for a year's free subscription!

But to return to my own experiences: I suppose my love of cricket blossomed in 1959 when I went to Australia with Eric. We went to see the Test matches every day, thrilled by the skills of Trevor Bailey, Freddie Trueman and Ted Dexter.

Ultimately our enthusiasm led to Eric and I forming our own team when we did a Blackpool summer season a year or so later. The team comprised stars from all the Blackpool shows of that summer, and we soon shaped ourselves into a fighting side – or so we thought! Our first game was against a team from a local school . . . and those schoolboys gave us the thrashing of our lives.

Of course, one of the advantages of being a showbiz cricketer is that you can get preferential treatment. It seems to be perfectly in order to approach the captain of the opposing side and say:

'Look, old boy, I'm working on stage tonight and it says in my contract that I'm not to be injured in any way. I can't put up with bruised legs or missing teeth. My smile is one of my greatest assets.'

That is one way of getting round the fact that basically I'm a coward, but occasionally such a technique works and the bowlers ease up a bit. I remember one particular occasion at a charity cricket match. It was agreed that I should be allowed to knock up a few runs to impress the fans. (Yes, there were a few.)

I had a marvellous time, and hit 35 in as many minutes. But my confidence got the better of me and, like a fool, I told the opposing captain that he could step up the pace a bit. He did. And I was out first ball.

One of the most important aspects of cricket is, of course, fielding. I usually go where the action is, and although that may sound a little odd, I have a very sound reason for choosing short leg, or the slips. The ball is usually flying off the bat at great speed and the chances of ever catching it (at least my chances) are almost impossible. Whereas if I were in the outfield and a batsman skied the ball, I would be a victim of that terrible hush that always falls around the ground, as I waited for the ball to come to me – knowing full well that I would drop it anyway!

Mind you, you get plenty of sympathy afterwards. People say 'Well you don't play very often' or 'The sun must have got in your eyes'. But that's small consolation if it's a cloudy day.

Yes, I love cricket, but I must stop trying to emulate the stylish batting of players such as Geoff Boycott and Tony Greig. It looks good, but I'm always bowled first ball. From now on, I will go out there and simply concentrate on hitting that damned ball . . . !

But whether you are a player of cricket or a spectator, it's a necessary concomitant to read some of the great literary pieces on the game. Every cricket enthusiast should have in his library the works of Sir Neville Cardus, R.C. Robertson–Glasgow, or the contemporary John Arlott. Plus, of course, a copy of *Wisden*. Mine has a prominent place on my bookshelf. Right next door to my ready reckoner!

A bat out of hell?

SIR LEONARD
HUTTON

Long Off

LORD'S: A YORKSHIREMAN'S VIEWPOINT

Generally speaking we do not care for Lord's. I myself for some years hated the place. The 0 and 1 which I made in my first Test match against New Zealand in 1937 did not increase my affection for the hallowed ground. A day or two before the Yorkshire team were due to make their annual pilgrimage to Lord's one could sense that most of the players would be pleased when the next match there would be over. I believe a Yorkshireman built the place, so why this awe, or fear, or hate, or dislike, which seemed to have inflicted itself on my boyhood heroes in the Yorkshire XI?

I wonder if the slope had anything to do with it; after all, other Test grounds the world over are flat by comparison with the Headquarters of Cricket. In later years I myself have developed a great fondness for Lord's. Having played there many, many times, I got to know the people who run the place, the gatemen, the groundsman, the cricket and administrative staff, but I never quite got to know the pitch. After all, you are bound to be suspicious of something that gave you a broken finger, and several other blows which I can clearly remember even though they are now of some thirty years standing. The behaviour of the crowd has always been impeccable, in direct contrast to that of the ball. There was the off spinner that Fred Titmus sent to me from the Pavilion End that pitched on my leg stump and hit the off. Then the leg break sent to me by Jim Sims from the Nursery End which pitched on my off stump and struck the leg stump. This is not nice, particularly when you return to the dressing room and a rough Yorkshire voice asks you, 'Where were your bloody pads'.

We normally used the dressing room under the pro's room, which is now a comfortable bar for the use of members. We had hard, upright chairs in our dressing room, which is now used as an office I believe. Two or three of the Middlesex players used this dressing room which I thought was odd, including Patsy Hendren. If you stood on tiptoe you could just see the match in progress, but only just. It was from this dressing room that Bill Edrich and I went out to face, although we did not know it at the time we put our pads on, the most ferocious piece of fast bowling that we had ever seen before or have we seen since. The match was the Gents v Players match of 1938. Ken Farnes, the giant from Essex, was the man who sent terror through the players' dressing room.

Bill Edrich took guard at the Nursery End to face Farnes from the Pavilion End; the time was 6.15pm. The first ball went very close to Bill's head, the second knocked him out, and he was duly carried off. Frank Woolley, playing in his last Gents and Players match, was captain. He had not seen the action, neither had Fred Price whom someone had suggested would make a good night-watchman. In 1938 we played the eight-ball over. Farnes' first delivery to Fred Price almost killed him – how that ball failed to remove Fred's head I will never know. Price growled down the wicket, 'What the bloody hell's going on here'. Fred survived another delivery, then decided this was no place for him at his time of life. He knocked the square leg umpire down before Farnes reached the wicket to deliver his next thunderbolt. Eddie Paynter then came out to join me; there were many other places where I would have preferred to be at that moment. Paynter avoided the three remaining deliveries, moving his head as a champion lightweight boxer would do. Farnes had bowled one over, the clock showed 6.30pm, and we walked slowly from the field. We thought of tomorrow, and of Farnes, who was in a savage mood having been dropped from the England team after his poor showing in the first Test match against Australia.

But to get back to my 0 and 1 in my first ever Test match. For the first time I was to use one of those luxurious dressing rooms on the first floor with sofas, and a perfect view of the game, very comfortable but not home to me. I would have preferred the old room with convenient access to the field, rather than have to walk downstairs, and through the Long Room on to the field.

In the preceding ten days I had made over 500 runs with Yorkshire, so there was every reason for me to feel full of confidence as I made my way through the W.G. Gates to start my Test career, but somehow I did not. Lord's that June morning seemed overpowering: a feeling of insignificance came over me, a feeling I still experience even today when I walk through those Grace Gates.

I settled myself in the strange England dressing room; such luxury I had never known before. This dressing room, I was to find out later, was the best in the world. I came to like, and even love it as the years rolled along.

Jim Parks of Sussex was my first England opening partner. I must admit I felt very apprehensive as we made our way down the stairs through the Long Room and on to the field. The first ball always worried me – would I see it, would it be straight? That morning at Lord's, Jack Cowie, one of the nicest fast bowlers ever, operated from the Pavilion End with the dark brick background which at the best of times was never ideal for batting. (Today I am pleased to say that some sort of a sightscreen has been erected which is a big improvement.) What confidence I had was quickly destroyed by Jack Cowie; and what a long way it was back to the pavilion. It was never ending. The same performance was repeated in the second innings, same bowler from the same end, time spent at the wicket almost identical in both innings. The England captain, R.W.V. Robins, said to me 'Whatever you do, don't do that against Australia next year'. This remark lifted me a little from the deep depression which had settled on me after my second failure. What would they say in Yorkshire, what would the Yorkshire team say when I rejoined them? One remark made by Maurice Leyland was 'Don't worry, Len, you've started at the bottom'. How true this was. I really liked that remark from Maurice, who made many classic statements on and off the field during his cricketing life.

I wonder as the years go by what has happened to the many people whom I have met during and after my playing days at Lord's. Yorkshiremen, Scotsmen, Australians, lawyers, doctors, painters, writers, musicians, opera stars, actors – from all walks of life you will find them at the home of cricket.

Shortly after the war, I think in 1947, a smart, well-attired gentleman came up to me in the pavilion and asked me if I backed horses. I did not reply, but I knew several people who liked a flutter. This stranger said to me that 'Friars Fancy' should win the 3.30 at Sandown Park. I returned to the Yorkshire dressing room with this useful information. Maurice Leyland was made thirteenth man due to a leg injury, so he decided to spend the afternoon at Sandown. I asked him to place a bet for me on Friars Fancy, adding that I thought the information was good. The horse won at four to one. The following morning I fully expected Maurice to produce the winnings, but instead he said how sorry he was that he had forgotten all about it!

On several occasions my contact at Lord's gave me very good tips. He certainly knew what he was tipping – I never knew his name, nor did I ever have but the briefest of conversations with him. Whenever we played at Lord's one or two players would ask me if I had seen that pal of mine. I wonder who he was, and where he is today – a winner would be very useful.

We also had our annual visitor from Los Angeles, who emigrated from London when very young. He was a fitness fanatic, and one of his interests was to keep film stars fit. He used to say to me that he could make me feel years younger. I listened to him carefully but I never felt any younger, or ran quicker between the wickets.

So to me Lord's was a ground I disliked in my early days, but as the years passed away I came to know the place and those who worked there and those who frequented the home of cricket. They became my friends, and from time to time their kindness has been overwhelming.

I have had some painful moments too. The one broken finger which I received was at Lord's, also the blow on my left thigh which I received from Gubby Allen in 1937. When the weather becomes cold and damp, my left thigh aches; that ball from Gubby which lifted and came down the hill, might have been bowled yesterday. The pain on the exact spot where the ball struck returns each winter to remind me of a fast bowler – and Gubby at his best was very fast.

Over the years we have seen many changes at Lord's. The new Winter Cricket School has meant that throughout the whole year, the sound of bat meeting ball can be heard. Long may it continue to be so, at one of the sanest places in the whole world.

Left: A great ovation from The Oval crowd in 1938, following Len Hutton's record innings of 364 against Australia in the Fifth Test. *Right*: In play against India in 1952, again at The Oval, where Hutton and Sheppard shared a record highest opening partnership for England.

E.W. SWANTON

Long On

A PLEA FOR PITY – AND A POSER FOR THE PUNDITS

Far be it from me, in the ordinary way, to criticise our captain, least of all so enthusiastic and agreeable a chap as Tim Rice. But to stick away out at long-on the oldest, heaviest, and no doubt the most decrepit member of the side touches – to quote Sydney Pardon on the selection of the England XI against Australia for the Oval Test of 1909 – the confines of lunacy.

Does he think I can run? Or throw? It'll be one for the hit, probably one for the fumble, and assuredly two for the throw: that's to say four. Better surely to tempt the lofted mis-hit by leaving the place untenanted, and add this willing but *passé* passenger to the infernal 'inner ring', and issue him with a pair of shin-pads – for use *under* the trousers naturally, *à la* the late Sir Julien Cahn.

But, supposing that my captain is unrelenting, I must take what comfort I can from the chance of finding some of the *cognoscenti* beyond the long-on boundary and engaging in a little 'urbane conversation' – as Neville Cardus of immortal memory once, curiously, described Warwick Armstrong's Australians as exchanging when they were walking out to field. (The phrase comes from his earlier writing pre-1936, that is to say before he had met many Aussies in the flesh.)

I might even find a member of the Cricket Society or some other obviously well-informed fellow who would relish the challenge of my stock 1978–79 question:

'Who was the touring captain who was also a musical composer with forty-two published orchestral works to his credit?'

'Was he an Englishman?'

'No.'

'A visitor to England then?'

'Yes.'

'By a side of Test standard?'

'Yes.'

(A long pause.)

'I give up.'

'Really – but surely you remember the Maharajah of Porbandar, who brought the first All-India side to England in 1932?'

I recall His Highness well, a figure of much dignity who with his aides and entourage made a stately progression round the country in a fleet of white Rolls-Royces. After playing in earlier fixtures he left the captaincy on the field to his vice-captain, Kumar Shri Ganshyamsinhji of Limbdi, who in turn often delegated the authority to that prince of cricketers, C. K. Nayudu.

Wisden summed up the delicate issue of the Indian captaincy on that first representative tour with its usual aplomb:

'Some little difficulty was experienced with regard to the captaincy, and after one or two disappointments the choice fell upon the Maharajah of Porbandar who had with him as vice-captain K. S. Ganshyamsinhji of Limbdi. For reasons apart from cricket, the necessity existed of having a person of distinction and importance in India at the head of affairs, and it was almost entirely because of this that Porbandar led the team. No injustice is being done to him, therefore, by saying that admirably fitted as he was in many respects for the task, his abilities as a cricketer were not commensurate with the position he occupied. Only those, however, with intimate knowledge of the many little difficulties arising in the command of a body of men of mixed creeds, habits and thoughts, can appreciate the tact and firmness required in maintaining that comradeship and united endeavour so essential to the success of a team on the field and the harmonious collaboration of its various units in other respects. Except for his limitations as a cricketer, the Maharajah of Porbandar enjoyed in full measure the attributes necessary to his position, and he certainly created in the team an excellent spirit.'

Now *there's* urbanity for you!

Porbandar batted three times in the first-class matches of his tour, and accumulated two runs. I always supposed I'd seen them both, scored to long-leg against Cambridge. But time plays strange tricks after forty years or so, and *Wisden* states categorically that at Fenner's he made a duck, having however scored two in an earlier game against Glamorgan at Cardiff.

What of his music? A good question which I can best answer by quoting from the current *Who's Who* entry:

'PORBANDAR, Maharaja of, Lt-Col H. H. Maharaja Rana Saheb, Shri Sir Natwarsinhji Bhavsinhji, KCSI . . . Captained 1st All-India cricket team which toured England 1932. Orchestral works published: 42 compositions . . . Recreations: Music, painting and writing.'

Not cricket! By the time this and perhaps other kindred esoteric matters had been exchanged with the spectators beyond the boundary, maybe an interval will have intervened – or, having ascertained that the Twelfth Man was on duty, I might have hobbled gratefully back in to the decent obscurity of the pavilion.

BRIAN
JOHNSTON
Slip

CRICKET HAS BEEN GOOD TO ME

An extract from Brian Johnston's speech at the Lord's Taverners Spring Lunch, 1979.

Mr Chairman, my lords, Lord's Taverners and guests. Cricket has been good to me, so I was both delighted and honoured when I received a letter from Tony Swainson inviting me to propose the toast of cricket at this lunch today. In fact I was so pleased that I rang him up that same afternoon to accept. However, one of those delightful secretaries down at the Lord's Taverners told me that he was not in the office.

'Oh', I said, 'doesn't he work in the afternoons?'

'No', she replied. 'It's the *mornings* he doesn't work. He doesn't come in in the afternoons.'

Anyway, as I said, I was so glad to be asked, because it gave me the chance to say thank you to so many people – people who have helped me and been my friends during my life-time of cricket. I'd like to start with my two cricket heroes. In 1921 I adopted Patsy Hendren, and from then until he retired in 1936 I followed his every innings and suffered moments of elation or despair depending on his form. Luckily it was usually the former. He was a lovely character and a great humorist and clown. He once told me that on Arthur Gilligan's tour of Australia in 1924 he was fielding in the deep down by the 'Hill' at Sydney. T.J.E. Andrews was batting and hit a ball in Patsy's direction miles up into the sky. Patsy positioned himself underneath the ball as it descended from a great height. A voice from the Hill shouted: 'Patsy, if you miss that catch you can sleep with my sister.' I asked Patsy what happened. 'Well', he said, 'as I hadn't seen his sister I decided to make the catch'!

When Patsy retired, it was inevitable that I should make his young protegé, Denis Compton, my new hero. And thank goodness I did. He gave me fifteen years or more of utter magic and I shall always be grateful to him. When he retired he joined us in the television commentary box, and what fun we had. The only trouble was that Denis has a dirty mind and an even dirtier laugh. The result was that a perfectly innocent remark could be turned into something rude, when accompanied by a burst of Denis's laughter from the back of the box. I remember once at Worcester I said: 'Welcome to Worcester, where you've just missed seeing Barry Richards hit one of Basil D'Oliveira's balls clean out of the ground.' A perfectly innocent remark in itself, but Denis's laugh conjured up thoughts of a remarkable but very painful feat.

On another occasion Derek Underwood had some batsman plumb out lbw. Everyone appealed and Charlie Elliot had no hesitation in raising his finger to give him out. 'Plumb out', I said. 'No one was in any doubt here. And I bet that all your fingers went up at home as well.' Once again a laugh from Denis helped to ruin my reputation.

I should like now to thank George Hirst, that loveable Yorkshire all-rounder who coached me at school, and off whom I once made a leg-side stumping which I shall always remember. You will, I'm sure, know that in one season he made 2,000 runs and took 200 wickets. When asked whether he thought anyone else would ever repeat the feat (they haven't) George replied: 'I don't rightly know. But what I do know is, that if anyone *does* do it, he'll be mighty tired.'

Next I am grateful to my Sealyham dog, Blob, who used to accompany me to all my cricket matches. When I was in the field he was quite happy just to sit and watch. Then, when we came off, he would run to meet me and carry my wicket-keeping gloves back to the pavilion. We soon gave him the nick-name of Larwood, because he had four short legs and his balls swung both ways.

I owe a debt of thanks to all the schoolmasters who helped and encouraged me when I was learning to play. None of them, thank goodness, was like the cricket master at Gilbert Harding's school. He thought he would get his own back on Gilbert, because the headmaster had said that Gilbert could go for walks instead of playing cricket. The reason for this was that Gilbert was fat and short-sighted. But it infuriated the cricket master than anyone should be allowed to miss cricket – however bad they might be. So when he was choosing the sides for the annual match between masters and boys, he put down Gilbert's name as one of the umpires. So reluctantly Gilbert put on the white coat and when the masters batted, the cricket master hit the boys' bowling all over the field. He had reached the nineties when a bowler at Gilbert's end hit him high up on the left tit, and stifled an appeal for lbw. But not before Gilbert had raised his finger and given him out. This infuriated the master, who, as he passed Gilbert on the way to the pavilion, said:

'Harding. You were *not* paying attention. I wasn't out.'

Gilbert thought for a second and then replied, 'On the contrary, sir. I *was* paying attention – and you weren't out!'

And now I should like to thank all my colleagues at the BBC who have put up with me for so many years. I'd like to start with John Snagge, who, many of you may not realise, did quite a bit of cricket in the thirties. In the summer before the war he was reading the news and giving the cricket scores:

'Yorkshire 234 all out' – he read – 'Hutton ill – no. I'm sorry. Hutton 111.'

Then there's Jim Swanton – the only man I know who, when it was raining at a cricket match, used to get into his Jaguar and switch on the windscreen wipers, so that people could see *him*. We used to pull his leg unmercifully. He and I were doing the television commentary at Lord's during that marvellous Test against the West Indies in 1963. At the same time, large crowds were gathering in St Peter's Square in Rome waiting for the white puff of smoke from the Vatican chimney which would announce the election of a new Pope. We were told that the cricket commentary would be interrupted for a special outside broadcast from Rome as soon as this white smoke appeared. But luckily whilst commentating I spotted that one of the chimneys on the Old Tavern had caught fire and black smoke was belching out. Our producer Anthony Craxton quickly directed a camera on to it and I was able to announce: 'There you are – Jim Swanton has just been elected Pope.'

Then of course there's John Arlott, whose Hampshire burr brings the smell of new mown grass and bat oil into your homes. And all the others including Freddie Trueman, who is such a great asset to us in the commentary box. He is especially helpful when it is raining and we carry on a chat show, instead of returning to the studio. Two years ago at The Oval he filled in time by asking us what was the fastest thing on two wheels in London. Needless to say we didn't know. 'An Arab riding a bicycle through Golders Green' was his answer.

Then I'd like to thank all the great writers who have given me so much pleasure, Neville Cardus, 'Crusoe' Robertson-Glasgow, Ian Peebles and so on. And of course the late L.N. Bailey of *The Star* who once wrote that a batsman had been clean bowled by a ball which he should have left alone. Or his namesake Les Bailey, poet extraordinary to the Wombwell Cricket Lovers' Society. After the streaker incident at Lord's, he sent me this poem:

'He ran on in his birthday attire
And set all the ladies afire.
But when he came to the stumps
He misjudged his jumps –
Now he sings in the Luton Girls Choir.'

Special thanks, too, to all my friends the cricketers who have always been so kind and friendly to me – a mere amateur. Cricket produces so many characters like George Gunn, Alec Skelding and Bomber Wells. So many stories one could tell. But one of my favourites is when Bomber at number eleven joined George Emmett, who was 95 not out. They got in an awful muddle over a run and in fact were running level in the same direction for what could have been the third or fourth run – no one knew, they were all laughing so much. George Emmett, a bit exasperated with his eye on his hundred, shouted to Bomber:

'For Christ's sake call, can't you.'

'Heads', said Bomber, as he struggled up the pitch.

I'm also particularly pleased to be able to thank Don Wilson – now the Head Coach at Lord's. He has always played cricket as it should be played: whether out in the middle, coaching small boys at which he is a genius, or singing over a drink after the game. He, like me, thinks that cricket is fun and we are all, I'm sure, very grateful to him for the pleasure he gives us. He's a kind person too, though on one occasion, he was a bit *too* kind. It happened on Ray Illingworth's tour of Australia when the MCC team were travelling up to Newcastle by train. A girl was nursing a baby in one of the carriages; the only other occupant was a man who kept staring at the baby. He just couldn't take his eyes off it, and the girl became more and more embarrassed and annoyed. Finally she could stand it no longer and asked the man why he was staring so. He replied that he would rather not say. But when the girl persisted he said he was sorry but the baby was the ugliest he had ever seen in his life. This naturally upset the girl who broke into floods of tears, and taking the baby she went and stood out in the corridor.

She was still crying when the MCC team came along on their way to the restaurant. They all passed her except for Don who stopped to ask her why she was crying. She told him that she had just been upset by a man in her carriage. Don told her to cheer up. 'I'll bring you back a cup of tea from the restaurant car. That should make you feel better.' So off he went and returned in about five minutes. 'Here's your cup of tea', he said to the girl, 'and what's more I've also brought a banana for the monkey!'

Finally I must apologise to all who listen to our Test match ball-by-ball commentaries for the way they put up with my many gaffes – none of them, I assure you, made on purpose. My most recent one was last season at Leicester where I greeted listeners with: 'Welcome to Leicester – where Ray Illingworth has just relieved himself at the Pavilion end.'

I would like to end with one very special word of thanks to our Founder – dear old Martin Boddey, who over a drink with his friends at the Lord's Tavern was inspired to think up this marvellous idea of the Lord's Taverners. It has given all of us who love cricket the chance to put something back into the game we love so much and which has done so much for us. So thank you Martin and those friends of yours. I would like to propose the toast of *Cricket* – coupled with the name of Martin Boddey.

CARDEW
ROBINSON
Gully

THE CRICKET BAT

I'm a cricket bat, a cricket bat
Is what I'm proud to be.
My father's Stewart Surridge
And my mum a willow tree.

My single life time mission
Which of course is known to all
Is to smite my mortal enemy
The hard cruel cricket ball.

Balls – how I love to smash 'em,
Balls – to frustrate and to foil,
As they try to hurry past me
Or try sneaking past – with guile.

And believe me, I can do it,
Be I called on soon or late,
Just provided that my master
Lets me stand up nice and straight.

I'll send that round red rotten thing,
Just where it ought to go,
If I'm only standing upright
With my face toward the foe.

And that, for many happy years,
Is just what I have done,
Because my batsman owner
Was an England number one.

But one day, to my horror,
This base, ungrateful star
He signed my chest and gave me
To a charity bazaar.

And if that wasn't bad enough,
(Thrown out by number one)
I'm bought by a Lord's Taverner
Who only plays – for fun!

Where once I stood up proudly
Waiting each ball to be struck.
I now lean limp and loosely,
Like a badly ruptured duck.

Balls; now they all get past me.
Balls; whenever they do please.
Balls with leers and balls with sneers
All balls; with ball faced ease.

And when I get within a mile
Of those red pesky things,
They always find my edges,
Or my oil hole, where it stings.

So now I'm a sad picture
In a bad state of decay,
A bat with battered edges
With my oil hole worn away.

A far cry from that bat I was.
'Cos now I know full well,
The bat I most resemble
Is a bat straight out of hell.

My appearance at the wicket
Now brings tears to purists' eyes,
I once so firm and rigid,
Like a lucky bride's first prize.

The effect upon my owner,
Every day more clearly shows,
Yes my sale brought him no century,
As only Parsons knows.

WILLIAM
RUSHTON
Square Leg

BATTLE OF THE GIANTS:
Corfu v Taverners

Nicholas Parsons said: 'Can you come to Corfu in June? Be filmed playing cricket for the Taverners? Bring the family. Stay the week. Two large ouzos please, Brenda.'

So there I was sitting on the north of Corfu enjoying a Fix and The Best of Patrick Campbell. Not the Fix that springs from a hypodermic, but a long, cool refresher with curious properties – not unlike Patrick Campbell. The hostelry was, as advertised, 'ALKINOO'S PLACE. GREEK FOOD. GREEK DANCE. ALKINOOS THE BOSS WELCOME YOU'. The family, being in the main Australian, were stretched out like lizards basking on a dusty beach, while I kept a weather eye on Albania and said Fix. It was halfway through the second bottle that I became aware that I was privy to an unnatural phenomenon. Albania was doing a Brigadoon. Prior to my first mouthful, Albania had been clear as a bell and some three miles across the bay. Now it was hardly there at all. I finished the glass and it disappeared totally. In the hands of the wrong sort of people and regularly fuelled with Fix, I could be a more potent force than the neutron bomb.

What, you are asking, has this to do with the Taverners and cricket? Great Powers! I cry, leaping to my feet, I had utterly forgot there's team practice on the ground at 3.30pm. I was back in Corfu town in but half-an-hour and a couple of punctures.

The Platia Down, the Corfu cricket ground, is half Fuller's Earth dotted with grass-like tufts, and half failed tarmacadam. (Not wholly unlike that pitch in New York on which Tony Greig's World All-Stars were wiped by a team of local cabbies and pushers.) The earthy area is next to the Judas Trees, under which the natives anxiously worry at their beads, sitting at tables served from the cafés behind them. These are set in a Rue de Ravioli-style arcade, built by homesick Frogs during Napoleon's better moments to remind them of Paree. The old Royal Palace stands behind the bowler at one end, the bandstand is at the Park End. On the Mediterranean side is an ancient fort and said tarmacadam, which fills as evening approaches with charabancs, a further hazard for the deep fielder, already tip-toeing through the pot-holes. Do not ask a man to drink and field square-leg.

The most sensible decision reached at the practice, as it transpired, was that John Price should do the batting as well as the bowling. He seemed the only one of us to have the measure of the mat, which had clearly been knitted by retired fisher-folk – not that it would have trapped anything less than something the size of Jaws, or indeed John Price. The only other cheery prospect for the morrow was that Ken Barrington (or *Captain* Barrington as the Greeks insisted, the officer young subalterns were warned against in the Mess in Old Delhi) had found his wicket at last. Anything he pitched on it turned three yards in either direction and bounced scalp-high. The ground had apparently been flattened by countless feet of Regiments of Foot in the halcyon days of Empire, and never since. Any hopes that the mildly apprehensive non-cricketers might have harboured – for example that the day would be light-hearted, that small jokes re the use of the heavy Hoover in the Ouzo-Interval could be bandied to the camera – were shattered when a deputation of grim-faced

Greeks arrived. They bearded Parsons (not Greek Orthodox priests – they seized Nicholas by the lapels) and announced that if as they had heard rumoured Roy Kinnear was to come in to bat on a donkey, there would be a walk-out and an International Incident of some proportions. We gathered that they take their cricket seriously, or not at all.

That evening there was a reception in a most gracious room in the Town Hall, the very room in which our Twelfth Man was christened. As Corfu was under the impression that they were playing England or at least the House of Lords, all the brass was assembled. The Governor, the Lord Mayor, the Fire Chief, the Police Chief, an Archbishop so venerable he could well have held the infant Twelfth Man over the basin, an Admiral dressed by Nathans, and for all one knew behind their dark glasses, the local Captains of Industry, Secret Police Chiefs and the Mafia. There was almost another incident.

The Taverners and their ladies sat in rows on one side of the room, the Corfu Brass against the opposite wall, the camera roamed between. John Cleese was positioned facing the white-bearded Man of God. After the ouzos and the *canapés*, there were the speeches, clearly meat and drink to the Lord Mayor who rose and in deep and volatile Greek proceeded to welcome us most warmly, or so we gathered from the extremely game attempt at interpretation by the tourist board chief. He, alas, pausing now and then to search for the *bon mot*, and despite interesting suggestions shouted across the room by the Admiral, began to fall some distance behind His Worship who was warming to his task in no uncertain manner. The race was on.

Then I noticed Cleese. Under the stony gaze of the Archbishop, he had begun to judder uncontrollably. The veins stood out on his noble head. Hysteria undoubtedly had him in its grip. I think it was the third reference to the Duke of Endema that almost did for him. His face shifted to purple, and hot tears poured down it. In the wake of the Scottish debacle in Argentina ('I'll have a Large Peruvian and Soda, please') there was talk of his being sent home early to be interviewed by Frank Bough re his shame. Happily it was all put down to sun and the emotion of the occasion, but it was a close call. No one corpses like Cleese. His giggle can down a bat at three hundred yards.

Saturday the tenth of June was bright and very hot. The opening ceremony was unashamedly based on that used in Buenos Aires to start the World Cup off and cheer up the regime. 'The Lord's Taverners', we were told, 'will follow the Boy Scouts'. 'Only so far' we cried, forming twos in a most military manner. The Scouts were between us and a sizeable band, brass helmets and sun-glasses gleaming in the sun. Behind us came the Sea Scouts and the Island's three cricket sides, elegantly track-suited and banners flapping. The crowd seemed enormous and evenly divided between our own tourists waving Union Jacks and light ales, and the locals thirsting for blood. Ours.

You'd have been proud. The Taverners marched on to the ground, chests out, stomachs in, whistling *Colonel Bogey* to a solo kettledrum. The national anthems were played. More speeches. His Worship was seemingly even more at home in the open, and gifts were exchanged, beer-mugs for tasteful medals. Then battle commenced.

The details of the game are lost I fear in Fixy mists. Perhaps because it was a Saturday it could certainly not be described as a Charitable Match. We realised at once that the Corfu Select XI was keen to rub our faces in the Fullers Earth. They batted first in a style all their own. The defensive stroke is not so much a dead bat as a dead body. Indeed the crack as one opener played John Price with his elbow caused several of the local gendarmerie to reach for their Lugers. Anything hittable was vigorously scooped somewhere in an arc between square leg and square leg. It was all effective stuff however, and given the old Taverner tradition of two overs each, slightly amended to give Big John exercise and to keep their score somewhere within the bounds, they scored something in the region of 220 as far as I can recall. Which is no distance whatsoever. We fielded with some distinction and our most successful bowler was Kinnear. He approaches the wicket at an angle of 90 degrees, moving uphill as if in the teeth of a force nine gale. He lobs left-handed with devastating effect. One unfortunate batsman turning quickly to alert the slumbering square leg umpire that a *bombada* or full toss was hovering somewhere above his stetson, trod on his wicket and was '*sotto*' – or out. Two others fell in sheer bewilderment at the dazzling mix of *bombadas* and devilish *primo slacos* or long hops. The donkey was avenged.

The task was formidable, but Captain Barrington was determined to win, and the general feeling was that he was right. Queen and country called. Corfu were taking no prisoners. Not for them our idiot tactic of sharing the bowling round. Their captain and another bowled short and briskly throughout. Thank God for the pros. Jack Robertson made an impeccable few, Ed Stewart and John Alderton thumped cheerfully, but it was a cracking 50-odd against the clock and a towering 120-odder from John Price that brought a famous British victory. The Greeks admitted they had never seen the like and the total runs scored in the afternoon broke all existing Island records. John, having opened and scored a century, at Edgbaston a week later batted fourteenth for the Taverners. Cricket's a fickle game.

There was a wild taverna (no relation) party under the brutal lights of the Parsons' film unit, during which almost the entire cast of Taverner's ladies limped from the dance floor as if they'd been playing Manchester at home, and Jolly Jack Alderton, in a fit of machismo, karate-chopped a plate and had to retire to a local maternity hospital to have his hand sewn back on. 'We don't do hands' said an unwilling gynaecologist, but every man has his price.

Team: Captain Barrington, John Price, Jack Robertson, John Alderton, John Cleese, Peter Gordeno, Nick Parsons, Brian Rix, Willie Rushton, Bill Simpson, Ed Stewart, and Roy Kinnear (3 wickets).

(This memorable match was the subject of a special Taverner film, produced by Nicholas Parsons and distributed by the Rank Organisation. It is now on general release. Ed.)

BARRY CRYER

Googly

THE DAY B.J.T. CAME TO BOWL

(with apologies to Marriott Edgar and Stanley Holloway)

There once was a fellow called Albert
A cricketer dashing and bold
Or to be more correct I'll say 'batting and bowled'
For there hangs a tale to be told

Now Albert was courting a lady
A lass by the name Rose Ann Kate
And she never stopped praising her idol
The great B.J.T. Bosanquet.

Yes – him as invented the googly
The off-break that's bowled as leg-break
And Albert got fed up about it
And used to cry: 'For heaven's sake!

'I'll acknowledge the man is a marvel
Some would say he's a right pioneer
But there's bowlers down here in the village
I will claim without favour or fear

'Who can sling 'em down twisting and turning
And spinning and breaking and that'
Said Rose: 'Now then Albert, let's get one thing straight,
When you mention the master – doff hat

'B.J.T. Bosanquet is a wonder
A man who is equalled by none
And if he came down here to the village
Not one of you'd muster a run'

'You're on!' cried our Albert with passion
'Let him bowl at our lads – every one
And when he gives up, we'll all show him
Exactly how it should be done'

'You're a dreamer, our Albert, you're potty!'
The sterling Rose Ann Kate then cried
'You seem to think bowling, like life, lad,
Is nobbut a bit on the side'

So they posted a letter to London
Inviting the great man to tea
Then added: 'PS If you'd like to join in,
We're having a knock – kick-off three'

Well, imagine their trembling excitement
When an envelope dropped on the mat
Inside was a note from the great B.J.T.
Saying: 'Thank you – I'll have some of that'

The great day arrived – it were sunny
And the lads of the village stood round
And somewhere a curlew were singing
And the landlord's dog peed on the ground

Then up drove a car – it were splendid
And the lads all craned forward to see
'By gum!' cried the vicar, 'Have you seen t'licence plate?'
And there was inscribed 'B.J.T.'

The king of the seam then dismounted
To a spirited round of applause
And Rose cried: 'You're welcome sir – teach 'em to win!
They'll tell you that I can't stand draws!'

So the stumps were set up in the sunlight
And then the great contest began
B.J.T. from both ends – every over
And the village turned out to a man

It took him ten minutes to do it
On the scoreboard it said: 'All out – Nowt'
And they carried him shoulder high after
And he said: 'Come on lads, it's my shout!'

And they laughed and they sang in *The Packhorse*
And they supped the ale all night in bulk
And only one man were nowhere to be seen
'Cos Albert had gone home to sulk

Now the ending of this stirring saga
Was that B.J.T. drove home to cheers
And the lads to this day talk about it
As they sup their Old English keg beers

'But what of our Albert?' you ask me
'Did he make young Rose Ann Kate his wife?'
No, she married the milkman, so he shot himself
I know it's right sad – but that's life.

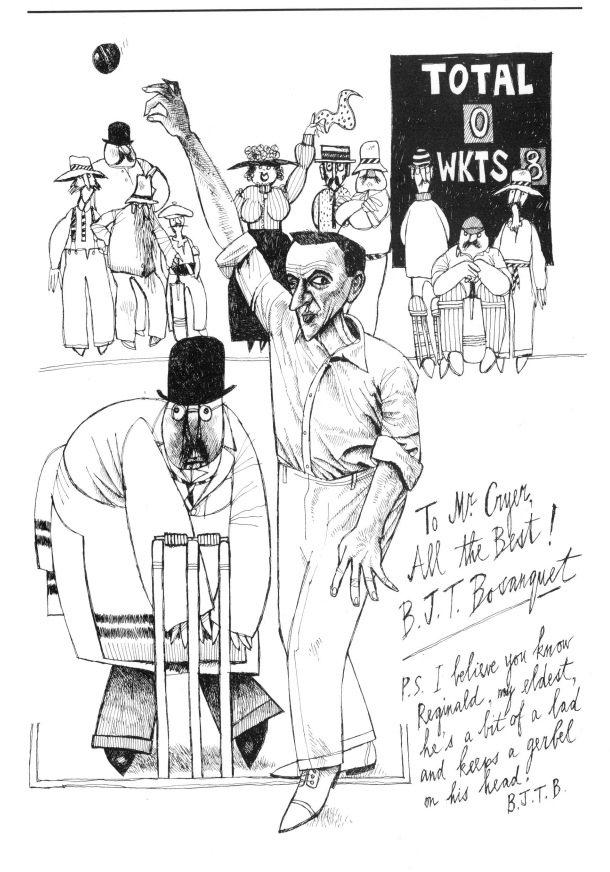

To Mr. Cryer,
All the Best!
B.J.T. Bosanquet

P.S. I believe you know
Reginald, my eldest,
he's a bit of a lad
and keeps a gerbel
on his head!
B.J.T.B.

JIMMY HILL

Offside

A PERSONAL EXPERIENCE

I remember only too well the day I returned as an ex-Fulham player, to Craven Cottage, to play with some of my ex-colleagues, now middle-aged, against the then Fulham first team for the George Cohen Testimonial Fund.

The 'old boys', giving away something like ten to fifteen years a man, began to perform surprisingly well. To their own astonishment, as well as that of the crowd, they took the lead. The Fulham lads began to get rather edgy, realising that the boys of the old brigade were not going to relinquish their one-goal advantage without a fight.

Suddenly, Bobby Robson broke through on the right of the goal, and shot fiercely against the goalkeeper's feet. The ball spun wickedly in the air in my direction, at an angle about fifteen yards from goal. I knew that I had to volley it: only a coward would have shirked that responsibility, and there was no way I wanted to be accused of that. So, doing my best to ignore the fact that the chances of me hitting the goal must have been around twenty to one, I closed my eyes and lashed at the ball. To my complete astonishment, it flew into the back of the net without the goalkeeper moving an inch.

I had never volleyed a ball more sweetly in the twelve years of my professional career. Once the crowd had recovered its composure after this extraordinary happening, a long suffering supporter was heard to remark in the stands:

'It's a pity they didn't bloodywell play like that when they were here.'

You can't win with crowds, can you?

A PERSONAL ENGLAND VERSE (to the tune of some familiar *My Fair Lady* music)

All we want is a pitch somewhere
A ball that's round and a ref that's square
To play without a care
Oh, wouldn't it be luverly
Lots of goals from the forwards' feet
Lots of scoreboards that say 'clean sheet'
Add up to victory sweet
Oh, wouldn't it be luverly.
Oh, so luverly dribbling down the field to score a goal
And when Kevin shoots it's always –
Right in that little 'ole
Skipper Em' says they should not pass
If they do they'll end up on – the grass
Did I say grass – what farce – oh, wouldn't
It be luverly, luverly, luverly . . .

MAX
BOYCE
No Ball

Anyone who has tried to get a ticket for a rugby international at Cardiff knows how difficult it is. My Uncle Will, however, got into the ground without a ticket dressed as one of the St Alban's band (the band that play at Cardiff Arms Park prior to the internationals).

The trouble was, all Will's friends and family got to hear of it ('cos he told Florrie Thomas not to tell anybody) and when the next international was due to be played at Cardiff, they all wanted to go as well.

The Incredible Plan, therefore, is the story of what happened . . .

THE INCREDIBLE PLAN

There's a story that's told in the Valleys
And I'll tell it as best as I can
The story of one Will 'McGonagle' Morgan
And of his 'Incredible Plan'.
It all started off on a cold winter's night
A night that was strangely so still
When the Rugby Club's General Committee
Banned *sine die* their ticket Sec, my Uncle Will
(Mind you, he was in the wrong, we knew all along)
There was no point in petitions or pickets
He was caught with this woman at the back of the stand
With the Club's allocation of tickets
And what made it worse, she wasn't the first.
He'd been caught with Ben Walters' wife Ethel
We all knew her with her fox and her fur
She used to wear on Sundays to Bethel
Anyway, Will was banned *sine die* – he broke down and cried.
I've never seen a man in such sorrow
'Cos like Judas of old he'd sold more than gold
With the Scotland and Wales game tomorrow
Then he had this idea: he'd go in disguise.
He had it all drawn up and planned
And he went to the game (to his family's shame)
As one of the St Alban's band
Back in the village they all got to know
'Make one for me' they'd all say
There was such a demand, it got a bit out of hand
He was making about fifty a day.
So he put an ad, in the *Guardian*
To employ a few men starting Monday.
And he did, he started some men – I think about ten,
On three shifts, and some working Sunday.
They made about three or four hundred
When the night shift were sent two till ten.

The jigs were all changed, the tools rearranged,
And they started on ambulance men!
Then they ran out of buttons and bandage –
And policemen were next on the plans.
Whilst 'B' Shift made refs with dark glasses,
Alsatians, white sticks and tin cans!
Then production was brought to a standstill
And the Union could quite understand
When management tabled the motion:
'Things are getting a bit out of hand'.
I'll never forget the day of the match,
The likes of I'll ne'er see again.
I can see them all still coming over the hill:
Hundreds and thousands of men!
The refs came in four double-deckers;
It was going exactly to plan.
And the St Alban's band came in lorries
And the police in a Griff Fender van!
No I'll never forget that day of the match,
The likes of I'll ne'er see again,
When Queen Street was full of alsatians
And the pubs full of ambulance men!
It was then I saw Will for the first time:
I was standing on the steps by the 'Grand'.
He was in a camel-hair coat (dressed up as a goat)
Marching in front of the Band!
It was then that the accident happened –
The roads were all slippy and wet.
He was knocked down by a man in a greengrocer's van
And they took him to 'Davies the Vet'.
Now 'Davies the Vet' is a bit short-sighted:
He said 'I'm afraid it's his heart.
But he wouldn't have lived longer, even if he'd been stronger:
His eyes are too far apart!'
The funeral was held on a Monday
(The biggest I'd ever seen).
The wreaths came in four double-deckers,
And there was one from Prince Charles and The Queen.
(Sorry, from the *Prince of Wales* and the *Queens*!)
There were sprays from three thousand policemen,
And one from the St Alban's band.
And the bearers were refs with alsatians,
Dark glasses, white sticks and tin cans.
We sang at the graveside the old funeral hymns,
And we all went to comfort his son.
What made him sad, he said, was that Dad
Had died not knowing we'd won!

I couldn't sleep for most of that night,
I kept thinking of what he had said:
'Dad had died not knowing we'd won',
So I dressed when I got out of bed.
And I walked again to that hillside
To that last resting place on a hill.
It was all quiet save when I leant over the grave
And I shouted 'We hammered them Will!!!'
And that story is told in the valleys;
I've told it as best as I can.
The legend of one William 'McGonagle' Morgan,
And of his INCREDIBLE PLAN!

COLIN
COWDREY
Most Runs

SUCH A HARD BALL – BUT A GENTLE ART

Who was it that decided that cricket should be played with a hard ball? I have taken so many knocks myself that I feel I shall carry them with me into old age. It was a tragic mistake not to have a soft ball. Sir Robert Menzies once told the England team at one of those memorable dinners he used to give as Prime Minister, and on this occasion as our host at Canberra, that he had an unstinted admiration for Sir Winston Churchill: but there was just one reservation. Churchill's wide ranging attention for everything about the British way of life failed to embrace the game of cricket. At a very early stage in their relationship, Sir Robert asked to be excused so as to spend a few hours at Lord's. 'H'm . . . h'm . . . cricket . . . h'm, that damned hard ball game at Harrow' – and wandered off. Apart from the occasional grunt of approval whenever England were doing well, he was never known to take much interest. I sympathise with him over his fear of a cricket ball and a dislike of its hardness.

I remember opening the innings in a junior school match for nine-year-olds. It was a warm, bright, sunny day and the headmaster produced a new cricket ball. I had never played with a new ball before, and I was struck by the shiny, bright, brilliant red colour of it as I played it away for a single off the first ball of the match. The next ball was a very high full toss, dropping on to the stumps. My partner was completely bamboozled. He adopted what would have been rather a good stance and position for bringing down a high pheasant. It was no surprise when he missed the ball altogether, but something of a calamity when the ball dropped on to the bridge of his nose and broke it. There was a piercing yell and blood everywhere, and the poor boy was carried off to the local hospital. That incident was to give me a healthy respect for the hardness of a cricket ball and the injuries it can cause.

On an early visit to Canterbury, I remember watching Ray Lindwall bowl the first over of the match to Kent opening batsman Leslie Todd, a good player if not the most rugged in the face of fast bowling. Almost at once, he was struck full toss on the toe: a most painful blow. There was a half-hearted shout for lbw, but poor Leslie hopped around in agony for several minutes, and to everyone's astonishment hopped off the field. He had no intention of facing another ball from Lindwall, nor of making an appearance in the second innings. Perhaps he was a good judge.

Bouncers were scarce in my early years, and whilst I was always on the look-out for the odd one, I never had the feeling that the bowler was out to knock me over. It is not quite the same these days – I retired at just about the right time!

The 'bodyline' series started something in 1932–33 which, by general agreement, was buried until the sixties. The seed had been sown by Douglas Jardine and his deployment of Larwood and Voce, and the evil lay dormant. Then, as the wheels of commercial cricket started to gather pace, and there were richer rewards for winners, so inevitably the big strong men came into their own. Brute force began to replace old-fashioned skills.

The administrators have been slow to act, mainly because they have found it so difficult to frame a law which defines a bouncer. Sadly, the spinner has been less of an investment than the fast bowler mixing skill with intimidatory tactics. Protective clothing has become a must. I remember playing in a Test match when Denis Compton put just a pair of socks in his trouser pocket as a thigh pad, and he wore only paper-thin batting gloves. In today's game he would be a prime target and would need to take much more care – yet I cannot see him, or The Don, wearing special headgear.

The first thing one sees on the field at Lord's is a helmet. It is a sign of the times. I remember seeing a fielder at a very close short-leg position one over, and stationed at deep mid-off for the next. It happened to be a very cold day and the helmet may have served to keep his head warm: but there is something rather incongruous about a deep fielder wearing a helmet. This, of course, is one of the problems, for the umpires have made it clear that they will not act as parking spaces for unwanted helmets in the same way as they do for bowlers' jerseys.

On an even colder day a week later, at Chelmsford, Michael Denness produced a new model of helmet, something akin to a balaclava. It kept the head and ears warm and, I am told, is fully protective too. It is less unsightly than the helmet but still pretty unusual.

I could not help wondering what George Duckworth would have said if I had taken a helmet with me on board ship as we sailed for Australia on my first tour. This great Lancashire and England wicket-keeper was ostensibly scorer and baggage master, but he was much more than that. Having toured Australia on numerous occasions, and won friends in every cricket country around the globe, he was something of a PPS to the captain, a permanent *éminence grise*. To the young players, like myself, he wore a stern, forbidding mask, but beneath, the heart was warm, and I regarded him as father and friend. I'm sure he would have taken one look at the helmet as we sailed out of Southampton water, and I would have been made to feel so uncomfortable that I could guarantee that the headgear would be floating in the Channel long before we reached the Bay of Biscay.

The helmet is something of a disfigurement on the cricket field, although hapless batsmen in certain conditions could make a good case for wearing it. I can think of some desperately sticky wickets in Australia under a fierce sun where Hammond and Hutton played fine innings, but had nothing to show for themselves in the record book – and those innings will never be forgotten by those who watched them. I imagine that they would not have argued if the twelfth man had walked on the field with a helmet. No, my complaint is that the helmet should not really *have* to come into play. That it does do so, and is necessary, concedes that there is too much rough intent.

Violence is, sad to say, very much the order of the day, and shows itself more and more in competitive sport. Soccer has its moments from time to time, and more recently rugby has become outrageously rough. The biting of ears and the hideous scraping of boot studs to tear the skin off a face caught in the scrum are acts which are quite unacceptable; yet they have happened.

In the game of cricket, happily, I cannot remember one player striking another. The nearest to that can come when a bowler stands rather firmly on his follow through, directly in the path of the batsman running through and trying to turn quickly for a second. On occasions, when the atmosphere is charged, I have felt the sharp point of a bowler's elbow in the ribs, accompanied by a little word in the ear for good measure. More infrequently, it can happen that a bowler runs across the batsman's path in such a way that it is difficult for the umpire to gauge whether his baulking is accidental. Some years ago there was a rather indelicate incident when John Snow was to be seen in a fair shoulder charge with India's little opening batsman, Gavaskar, knocking him for six.

The only time I have ever really felt like moving into action myself has been when a fielder has come and positioned himself very close to me, square on the offside of the wicket. Such field settings are of nuisance value, and are placed to distract concentration. I would like to see this ruse outlawed, because there is no way that the fielder can keep still throughout, however hard he may try, and in moving he breaks the code which defines fair and unfair play. I have been tempted to let the bat go at the end of my stroke, but when it came to it, courage has failed me, and on reflection, I do not regret that.

Cricket has always been a peaceful game, with the emphasis on skill. In recent years, as commercial sponsorship has improved the reward for winning, it was only to be expected that players would press harder for victory. Bouncers, as a weapon of intimidation, do bring results, for no one likes being hit by a hard cricket ball. In the razzmatazz of World Series Cricket, fast bowlers bowling an unlimited amount of bouncers has made for more spectacular watching, yet to the cricket connoisseur, the development has been hard to bear. The cricketers themselves have not enjoyed it, I am glad to say. As a result, an experimental law has been introduced into English cricket for the summer of 1979 restricting bowlers to one bouncer an over, a bouncer being defined as a ball which rears over shoulder height when the batsman is standing normally. The umpires have been charged to interpret this new rule strictly for the good of the game and, indeed, to put the emphasis back upon skill rather than force.

Violence and strong-arm tactics may amuse those in front of the Tavern from time to time, but it is cricket as a game of skills that we must seek to promote and preserve.

JOHN
SNOW
Most Wickets

SOMETIME WHEN I'M OLDER

Sometime when I'm older
perchance my mind will range
over days when I was a cricketer
unaware of time's colder ways,
then perhaps in a dusty corner
amongst the jumble of life
I'll recover cobwebbed memories
of past summers and friendly strife.

The vicarage lawn and village green,
church tower shimmering in high summer scene,
honeysuckle days of horses pulling harvest machines,
backyard centuries and boyhood dreams.

Later, in far flung places, meeting idols galore,
F.S., George, Wes and many more,
playing amongst them, a minnow 'midst whales,
gathering impressions and numerous tales . . .

From clamouring Caribbean palm-fringed ovals
with Sobers strong and smooth as Mount Gay rum
casually batting rummaging through bowling
dimming even the tropical sun;
To writhing, wracking Bangladesh birth,
all riots hardship and blood on dry earth,
matches played on political whim,
Bhutto's anthem, Ayub Khan's funeral hymn;
Then schizophrenic Australians, bottles and cans,
Pommy bastard, 'on yer mate let's shake hands,
Lillee and Thomson, the Chappells and Co,
white flannelled undertakers happy you should go.

Laced through these winters, back at home,
County games, facts and figures for *Wisden*'s tome,
and Lord's on historic Test match days,
the 'Egg and Bacon' and traditional ways.

Finally, after it all, in later years,
games played to assuage some of life's tears
Lord's Taverners friendship, more fun and show,
hoping for others things we were lucky to know.

Sometime when I'm older . . .

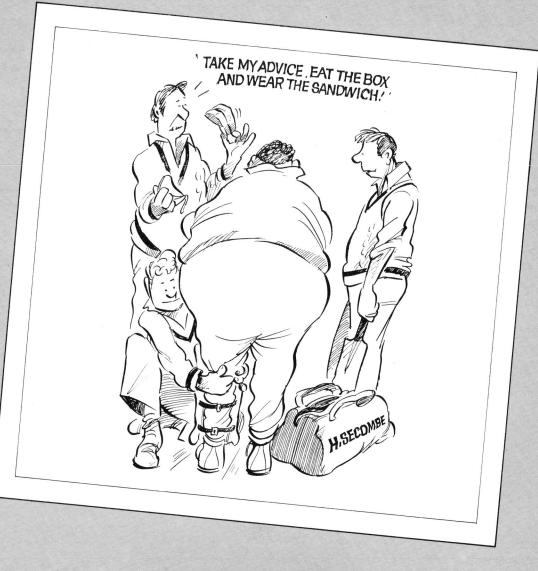

HARRY
SECOMBE
Wides

FAT CHANCE

I am probably the only man for whom a wide has been signalled by the umpire before a ball has even been bowled. I have also been described as a 'heavy roller to be used between innings' by one heavily jocular commentator, and asked if I would kindly loan my shirt for the purpose of a sight screen. At one time when I was batting with Colin Milburn at Bickley Park, someone claimed that as we ran between the wickets we registered seven on the Richter scale. These allusions to my weight and size were all meant in fun and I took no exception to them, but deep down I yearn to spring around the field like Derek Randall, bat with the confidence of Ken Barrington, and bowl with the dexterity of Derek Underwood. 'Fat chance', you cry, and well you may. But a man can dream.

Before the start of the first match of the season, in my mind's eye I can see myself striding towards the wicket, bat tucked firmly under my arm, the collar of my crisp, white shirt raised up to protect the back of my neck, pads gleaming, boots immaculate, cap tilted slightly at a jaunty angle. I take guard, pat the crease with authority, then take a cool look around at the field placings, smile slightly and prepare to face the first ball. The bowler rushes in, snorting like a bull, and whips his arm over savagely, releasing a bumper at my head. I pick it up immediately with my eye and, moving the feet at just the right moment, I hit the ball hard towards the boundary. The umpire's hands go up for six and the crowd goes wild.

Of course, it's never like that when the moment comes for me to bat in the first charity match in which I have been foolish enough to agree to play. I am usually in the beer tent telling lies about last year's matches when the captain comes running in to tell us that I'm in next wicket down. That's when the panic starts – it's been fun up to now, chatting with the famous cricketers, exchanging banter with the Bedsers, showing Colin Cowdrey how to handle his bat and making other endearing efforts to keep the team happy. Now the jig's up, my bluff is about to be called.

I've only got one pad, I discover, when I get back to the dressing room. 'Where's my box?' I cry, searching frantically in my bag through the debris of last season. I find it nestling among the remains of three cheese sandwiches which were freshly cut for lunch at the last match of last season. They don't look too good now and neither does my box. The elastic in my jock strap has stretched and when I put it on, the protection I need to cover my vital parts is perilously close to disintegration. The plastic cup is in two halves. I drag out my trousers, green-stained at the knees where I had fallen repeatedly to avoid encounter with balls driven at me by Micky Stewart. When I put them on, I find that they have shrunk since last year. They've spent eight months doing nothing in my bag – and now when I try them on the waistband doesn't meet. What mysterious shrinking propensities has my cricket bag developed during that time? The same thing has happened to my shirt: a light grey in colour (from a lack of sunlight perhaps), but the buttons refuse to do up. As I struggle into it the fleeting thought crosses my mind that perhaps I have put on a little weight. I dismiss the thought immediately. My boots, piebald with the years, are my next problem. The laces have so many knots in them that there is little lace left. I am assisted into my boots by those members of the team who are not rolling on the floor of the dressing room with laughter. A pad is found which does not match the one I have, but I am strapped into them both, leaving me to face the bowling with what appears to be two left legs. In the battle to dress I find that one half of my support is nestling against my right kneecap. I am about to retrieve it when we hear a great shout from the crowd.

'You're in next. Hurry it up', says the captain, coming in through the door. He sees me and collapses into uncontrollable mirth. I leave the dressing room feeling a little hurt, as I pull on a pair of batting gloves which have a net total of seven complete fingers and a wedge of cheese sandwich in the thumb.

I wave to the crowd, raising my crumpled Taverners' cap with one hand and gesturing regally with the other. When I get halfway to the wicket I realise why I have two hands free to acknowledge the crowd. I have no cricket bat.

'Mr Secombe is going to face the bowling single handed. With a figure like his they'll never see his wicket anyway', says jovial Alan Curtis over the loudspeakers.

A bat is produced by a member of the team, and I eventually arrive at the crease, heart pounding, a metallic taste in my mouth and my spectacles so steamed up that I can only just make out the opposite wicket. My support is now equally divided between my left knee and my right ankle.

Fred Trueman is called on to bowl to me – regardless of the fact that there are three balls to come from the local bowler. The crowd roars as Fred marks out his run, finishing up on the far boundary. I clutch myself nervously in the area where I feel most bereft. The rest of the side all get behind the wicket, leaving the field to Fred Trueman, the umpire, the other batsman, and myself.

'Great sense of humour has Fred', says the umpire, chuckling.

Fred begins his run and like a fool I stay at the crease. 'He'll drop the ball when he gets to the wicket', I think hopefully. 'We've had a lot of laughs, old Fred and I.'

He's still running and he hasn't dropped the ball yet. The crowd is hysterical. I am hysterical, but not with laughter. I don't see the ball leave his hand, all I feel is the impact of the ball on my instep. It flies to the boundary and the umpire signals four. I drop the bat and leap around on one foot. The crowd loves it, Fred loves it, and it takes four team members to carry me back to the pavilion.

That actually happened, and on cold winter's days I can still feel where the ball hit my instep. There's one consolation though: whenever I get together with cricketers I always say, casually, 'I once made a boundary off Trueman, you know – put him away to leg first ball.'

MICK McMANUS
Bouncer

A GAME FOR SOFTIES?

'I'm playing in a charity cricket match this Sunday – fancy coming along?' I asked a friend.

'Cricket? Bit of a soft game for you, isn't it?' Alex replied. I just shrugged my shoulders.

Sunday found us travelling down to Reading. We arrived, had a small beer, and then I got changed.

We won the toss and put the opposing side in to bat. The weather was beautiful and it was the usual light-hearted game – plenty of runs were scored and the wickets fell at regular intervals. Then number five arrived at the wicket – he was a hefty-looking lad. He proceeded to put bat to ball in no uncertain fashion.

Field placings in these games are not really important, and you tend to go where needed. I found myself at square leg. There was a change of bowling and a spinner came on, which suited number five down to the ground. He lobbed up a friendly one, the batsman took an almighty swing, connected, and the ball came towards me at a terrific pace. Had I had more sense, I would have let it spin harmlessly past, but I stuck out my hand in a vain attempt to make the catch. The ball caught the tip of my little finger and sped on to the boundary.

I looked at my hand to give it the usual magic rub, and noticed the tip of my finger was badly split and dripping blood. Wrapping it in a handkerchief, I made for the pavilion. A couple of officials had a look and decided that hospital treatment was needed, so I was driven off.

Fortunately the casualty department was empty, and I was ushered straight in to see a doctor.

'Been playing cricket have you?' he asked. 'I like a game myself. If I hadn't been working I would have come along.' His accent indicated he was Australian. 'The nail will have to come off in order for the finger to be stitched', he said. Charming, I thought.

A local anaesthetic was administered, and Aussie went to work. We discussed the international cricket situation at great length, and it was all quite painless – the nurse dressed the finger and I left with my arm in a sling.

We arrived back at the ground in time for tea, which was most welcome. Everybody was sympathetic and hoped I would be fit again soon. I got changed and watched the rest of the match from the comfort of a deck chair.

It wasn't long before the effects of the anaesthetic started to wear off and my finger began to throb. By the time I reached home it was going like a pumping station. I suffered considerable pain and discomfort for days, lost a great deal of sleep, and had to cancel some lucrative engagements.

A soft game, Alex? Give me wrestling any time!

Whatever happened to Frank Buck?

I've swallowed the ball

THE SMOKER

The 1.18 from Kings Cross to Bradford and Leeds connected with Wakefield, Halifax and most of the towns in that area. Consequently it was popular with the wrestling fraternity and there were always three or four of us travelling together.

On this particular occasion, the train was quite full, and the only way we could sit together was to occupy a non-smoking compartment. This didn't suit Jack, who was a compulsive pipe smoker. If he could have devised a way of smoking and wrestling at the same time, he would have done.

We settled down. A couple of people read books and papers and one dozed, while Jack, of course, lit up and puffed merrily away, filling the whole compartment with smoke.

It wasn't long before the ticket collector's voice came echoing along the corridor. Jack looked from the smoke, to his pipe, to the 'No Smoking' sign, and decided to act quickly. I was sitting opposite him and appeared to be asleep. So Jack placed his pipe beside my hand.

The ticket collector came in, saw the smoke and the pipe, and gave me a nudge.

'Sorry, Sir', he said. 'You will have to extinguish your pipe, this is a No Smoking compartment.'

I opened my eyes, picked up the pipe, and threw it straight out of the window. Jack just had to grin and bear it . . . !

ALL SMILES

Many wrestlers have their front teeth missing – it's an occupational hazard – and Cliff was no exception.

During a hectic match, his false plate with three teeth attached shot out of his mouth, and landed on the canvas in the middle of the ring.

Quick as a flash, Cliff did a quick forward roll, picked up his teeth, popped them back in his mouth and finished up on his feet, all smiles . . .

THE NAKED TRUTH

Most wrestling shows start between 7.30 and 8pm. The contestants are expected to present themselves at 7pm. On this occasion the train was delayed and I arrived at about 7.40. The programme that evening was due to commence at 7.45.

I was scheduled for the second match that evening, and had to get ready in a hurry. It is the policy to have all the men changed and ready in case the preceding match finishes quickly, because nothing is worse than the public having to wait a long time between bouts. The promoter was hurrying me up as the first match was due to start in a few minutes.

I stripped off and put on my dressing gown (this was in the days when long gowns were in fashion) and started to get my boots on. I had just about finished when the dressing room door burst open, and one of the officials called for the next pair. The first match had only lasted five minutes – one of the wrestlers sustained a badly cut eye and the referee had to stop the contest.

The promoter took a towel out of a bag, threw it to me, and hustled me out on my way to the ring.

My usual method of introduction to the crowd was to loosen my gown and when the MC said 'Mick McManus from New Cross' I would swing round, taking off my gown all in one flamboyant movement.

This time, just before the announcement was made, I looked down and to my amazement realised all I had on was boots, socks and gown! In the rush I had forgotten to put on some trunks. Quickly I tied the gown, mumbled to the second that I had forgotten my knee bandage, and beat a hasty retreat to the dressing room.

Can you imagine the public's reaction, had I whipped off the gown as usual? No doubt some would have sympathised, others commended me, and a few ladies might even have fainted . . . though not many I think.

PATRICK MOWER
Leg-Bye

WHY I TURNED TO CRICKET – OR CONFESSIONS OF A FOOTBALLER!

It all started with Mary Whitehouse. (I'd like to finish with her – but that's another story!) When I created a certain gentle, charming, fun-loving policeman in a television series called *Target*, Mrs Whitehouse and her strange bedfellows (the thought is horrifying) convinced the Elders of the BBC that my Detective Superintendent was really a violent, blasphemous, immoral thug. The newspapers, needless to say, thought this was great copy and eventually my 'monster' was banned from the tube – much to the distress of my mother, and J.N. from Wanstead.

Meanwhile, throughout this period, I had been following my obsession of trying to prove to various Round Tables, youth clubs, factories – in fact any group that could muster twenty-two legs – that Georgie Best and I had more in common than just being amazingly sexy and handsome! I was playing football. The teams I played for went under the dubious titles of Entertainers, Showbiz XI, Top Ten XI – *even* – and we are now reaching the point of this tale – even the Patrick Mower XI. Gosh!

I, being a striker (not the British Leyland sort, the goalscoring sort) usually managed at least two goals per match. This was achieved by a quick trip into the opposition's dressing room to inform their defenders that I was insured for £750,000, so would they 'watch the legs, and the face – shouldn't be playing really you know!'. It never failed. I would then perform my Nureyev jinks around the stationary defenders – whom the crowd believed to be mesmerised by my brilliance.

On the day in question, it was the PM XI versus a Police XI. Hmm! I thought it boded ill when in the bar at lunch-time, having my pre-match drink, I was nudged in the ribs (another sign I should have noted) by an enormous six-foot twelve-inch ex-boxer, who was glaring menacingly down at me. The following dialogue took place:

Him: 'You Patrick Mower?'

Me: 'Er, yes – that's right.'

Him: 'My wife thinks you're amazing.'

Me: 'Oh, that's nice.'

Him: 'Yeah! But I think you're a bleeding poof!'

Well, I mean – what could I say? I just picked up my handbag and left.

I did my usual pre-match grovel, noting that the two defenders were both Sergeants – and very big with it. Then I led the team out on to the pitch. The sight of my amazing legs brought the usual sighs and squeals of delight; the girls liked them too.

Then! Then followed the incident – in front of two thousand five hundred people – that finally persuaded me that I would be better pursuing a more sophisticated, gentlemanly game like cricket.

It was only the second minute of the game and I had the ball; which was unusual in itself. So I thought, 'I might as well score one of my goals now, and then I can hang about on the wing, chatting up the birds until half-time'. So off I went.

I think I was Johan Cruyff that particular afternoon, as I snaked effortlessly round the 'hypnotised' opponents to the delighted cries of:

'Go On Superintendent'

'Score a Packet Hackett'

or even 'Get A Hat-Trick, Patrick'.

I must have beaten at least thirteen players, when I saw I only had one person left between me and my goal. One of the Sergeants.

I tapped the ball with the outside of my right foot – Kevin Keegan now – and with a flick of my hips rounded my obstacle. At least I nearly did!

As I passed the stationary Sergeant, he leant back about four feet, and then launched himself at me like a Chieftain tank. He caught me in the ribs (remember?): just as my Bobby Charlton left foot was poised ready to explode the ball into the back of the net! Instead my whole body exploded about six feet in the air and I remember thinking 'I wonder if Rudi ever got this high?' before I crashed into a crumpled heap on the turf.

The crowd were in hysterics – laughter I'm afraid – as I lay looking painfully up at Goliath, who, with a beautiful smile, stepped over me and said:

'Sorry Pat. But I've always wanted to do that to a Superintendent!'

At the hospital, still caked in mud, I was informed that I had two broken ribs, a sprained ankle and variegated bruising. As I gazed self-pityingly in the mirror at my mud-blackened face I thought: 'I bet Gary Sobers never had this trouble.' Gary Sobers? *Of course* – Gary Sobers!

That's why nowadays you are more likely to find me trying to bowl the odd maiden over on the boundary, or thundering up to the wicket, steam coming out of my ears as I prepare to let loose my Freddie Trueman . . .

JOHN
CLEESE
Bowled

Long John Cleese?

Long Boat Cleese?

CHRISTOPHER
MARTIN-JENKINS
The Correspondent

GARDEN CRICKET

The garden of the first house I was lucky enough to own consisted of a long, thin stretch of weedy lawn, marked on one side by a tall privet hedge and on the other by an even weedier patch of mud which we were pleased to call 'the border'. Only a couple of apple trees and a fence broke the monotony, and there was no room for a cricket net.

Beyond the fence, however, lay the estate's sole redeeming feature, a babbling stream inhabited by mallards and occasionally on winter mornings visited by a stately heron, who was obviously under the impression that there was a fish to be had for breakfast, though I never saw one.

Around the time that our Editor (with a dictatorial authority which would have made Colonel Juan Peron look like a dithering and indecisive bureaucrat) was ordering me to produce something for this tome, I was revisiting this humble but happy home, having drinks with the present owners. It was spring, warm enough to sit outside by the stream, and we were watching the ducks enjoying their traditional seasonal frolics. (The drakes were enjoying it anyway. The female of the species seems to me to get a very raw deal: indeed, sometimes it's a wonder she is not drowned in the act.) I suppose it was a mixture of the sun and the ducks themselves which made me start thinking of cricket, or, to be more precise, of garden cricket.

I had better warn you now that this is going to be a childish indulgence in youthful dreams: for of all the cricket I have played, I think my boyhood games in a much larger and more interesting garden were the most satisfying, the most joyful, and certainly the most successful.

I suppose most boys who become infatuated with cricket at an early age dream of playing for their country, and no doubt most of them play imaginary Test matches. Not only was I no exception, but I actually spent the whole of my spare time playing garden cricket, except during blizzards and severe thunderstorms (but they had to be severe) when the game would be transferred to my bedroom and continued with a toy rifle as the bat and a ping-pong ball, which swung and spun devilishly.

I appreciate that even this all-consuming passion was probably far from unique, but what was different, I believe, about my games was the men who played them. You see, I genuinely had to imagine myself a real member of the England team and whereas others might see themselves playing alongside Hutton or Compton or Graveney or May, I found this too unrealistic. So instead I willed myself forward in time and invented the England team of the future, of which I was the charming, modest, talented and much admired captain.

In the great England side of this imagined era (I suppose logically, if I was to play a part, it should have been the 1970s, but in fact when I put a date at the top of a scorecard it was usually somewhere in the 2050s – a hundred years on.) In this side I was both opening batsman and opening bowler. I rarely failed to make a big score, and I played all the strokes although, for the sake of realism, I was not impregnable. The running commentary (by myself) which always accompanied the whole match, spoke of grace, power and enterprise. My driving had rarely been equalled in the history of the game. Peter May perhaps had been equally good on the on side; Len Hutton, Tom Graveney and Colin Cowdrey on the off; but few if any had achieved such an all-round mastery. If I did fail – and one played against some formidable overseas bowling – I usually made up for it with a devastating spell of outswing bowling. Some of the figures I achieved in Test matches were the equal of anything Spofforth, Barnes, Trueman or Lindwall ever produced.

But this was no one-man team. My opening partner was my brother, a plucky red-haired left hander. I used to think that he did not quite have the same natural ability, the same extraordinary power and range of stroke, but what a competitor, and what a prolific run getter! He *had* to be, for when I was not playing Tests by myself, he was playing them with me, and the game had to be interesting for both.

Number three: now that was a problem position. How many hours did the fraternal selectors spend, late at night, discussing who would do this important job best. No one ever quite established himself, but more often than not Robin Smaels, son of a man who had been Nottinghamshire captain at the turn of the twenty-first century, was chosen. Looking uncannily like M.J.K. Smith, he was a bad starter, but, if he got going a tall, elegant stroke player and also a very fine close fielder. Some newspapers annoyingly persisted in spelling his name Smales: it was not, it was Smaels.

Paul Gruché made number four his own. Here was a man with all the shots, another Denis Compton in his lifestyle and his batting style. About five foot ten, with strong wrists and shoulders, dark, casual, handsome – the son of a French actor, oddly enough. He played, by the way, for Middlesex, and I suppose, though quite unconsciously, he was modelled a bit on Compton.

At number five, Russell Prince. The name explained the man: regal, dashing, young, haughty. Although he played for several years, he remained the young promising member of the team, permanently in his third year at Cambridge, gloriously continuing the amateur tradition.

At six and seven came two more all-rounders: Calthorpe, a very swift opening bowler off a short run and a batsman who had genuine class; and Bob Crale, captain of Gloucestershire, a loyal man, red-faced, from a farming family; a lusty hitter and a steady medium paced bowler who could swing it both ways. A man who often came good in a crisis.

The spinners were not always the same. David Angus, Marlborough and Oxford educated, was usually the off-spinner, though he had not yet fully mastered the accuracy and the power of spin which had made his predecessor, Bill Brazier of Surrey, the best of his type since Laker a hundred years before. Brazier himself occasionally made an emotional comeback in my games.

Angus, by the way, played for Warwickshire. He rarely, if ever, went through a Test series with the same spinning partner (indeed he more than once lost his own place to Dicky Grenville, another off-spinner with a slinging action who spun the ball devastatingly but lacked control). The left arm rivals were Pullin of Gloucestershire and E.W.W. Macer of Derbyshire.

Pullin, with an action extraordinarily reminiscent of Johnny Wardle, usually got my vote. If a leg spinner was selected it was usually Billy Kent, an eccentric young Surrey player who was also a pop singer.

There was never any doubt about who should take the new ball. It had to be Mike Brackley, a Yorkshireman through and through; dark, rugged, outspoken, from mining stock of course. He used to be a bit of an embarrassment to me on tour sometimes, but Mike and I got on well and he was a ferocious bowler to have on your side.

As for the wicket-keeper, although in the twentieth century Kent might have enjoyed something of a monopoly, Lancashire took over in the twenty-first, because the three who held the spot during and just after my playing days were all Lancastrians: 'jumping' Johnny Vasser, his young brother Bob, and later, perhaps the most immaculate of them all, Ken Potter. Jumping Johnny Vasser got his name one summer holiday in North Wales, which my brother and I spent diving around in the sand dunes, taking brilliant catches with a hard little rubber ball from Woolworths.

These men lived for me, blissfully happy people who, even amidst the dreariness of a Latin or Maths period, could be called instantly to mind to relieve the boredom.

I still have scorecards of some of the Tests these imaginary men played, written on pieces of faded cream paper in a spidery hand with the ink often blotched by a passing shower. I have never had the heart to throw them away. Indeed, I am rather ashamed to admit that one or two of these names will be resurrected in a slightly different guise if Macdonald and Jane's, in their infinite wisdom (not to mention infinite *Wisden*) persist in their intention to publish a cricketing thriller of mine within the next few months. (The story starts just before the final Test of a series in the Caribbean and a few things happen off the field as well as on it – perhaps you will put it on your Christmas list for next year!)*

As for the garden cricket, I think I now have a lawn just about big enough for a Test match again and I am working on my own children in the hope that they will get the same innocent enjoyment from it that I have done. I just give them the odd subtle hint, such as buying them bats, balls and stumps, mowing out a pitch, and offering to play with them. You must never *force* your own interests on your children, must you?

* *(This is shameless advertising and out of order–Ed.)*

TONY
LEWIS
Extras

EXTRAS I HAVE KNOWN

The word extra, according to the *Oxford Abridged*, means 'situated outside of a thing; not coming within its scope', which, in my own cricket imagery, stirs up a memory or two.

Glamorgan, needing only 85 to beat Derbyshire at Chesterfield, somewhere in the mid-sixties, had reached the amazing total of 60 for 7. Alan Jones and I were unable to watch any more, indeed we could not even stay in the ground. So, situated outside it, i.e. not coming within its scope, we walked the pavements outside the walls licking ice-creams, listening to the delight inside as Glamorgan were tortured. We won in the end, but no thanks to the extras, Jones and Lewis.

To be exact we were extra-mural, but, let me think, that brings to mind a more illustrious occasion. England were playing India in a Test match at Calcutta. There were 85,000 Indians inside the ground at Eden Gardens, and 85,000 outside – because in accordance with a long-standing Indian practice, the tickets had been duplicated and sold twice. Extraordinary, or should I say, extraordinarius.

This meant simply that when the Indian players appealed against an English batsman for lbw, the 85,000 inside the ground appealed and so did the 85,000 extra-mural, who were by now listening on transistor radios – and you know how they qualified for those! (Well, at least it made their extramaritals a little less worrying.)

Unfortunately, those Indian umpires, subject to so much extra-cranial persuasion, looked shabbily at the turf, and raising a bent finger, mumbled the dreaded message 'I'm terribly sorry sir, that's out'. Absolutely extra-cosmical they are.

Of course, extras are in the hands, or rather out of the hands, of the poor wicket-keepers. My favourite 'keeper is Alan Knott. I was sorry when he went to Kerry Packer's World Series cricket. How can you have an identity when you are playing for The World? Who on earth do you play? Home matches against Mars and Jupiter? What a life poor Knotty had out there in Australia, condemned to play out his days in a pastel shade blue cap in some extra-terrestial fixture list. What satisfaction is there as a mercenary performing in an extravaganza set up by a millionaire extrovert?

Still, Mr Extravert proved beyond doubt that the Boards of Control were acting in an extra-judicial way towards our cricketers. Now, at least, they have some pocket money for a beer at weekends.

Ah! Talking of extrovert millionaires – shall we ever see Tony Greig again? He is tucked away in a lavish retreat in Sydney. I last saw him as a cricketer, helmeted, in one of the World Series floodlit night-matches. I don't think he saw me, his face was blinkered by the headgear and his visor dazzled. I was extra-spectral as far as he was concerned. Only extradition will bring him back . . . like Ronald Biggs I guess, from Brazil.

In the same way our editor, Tim Rice, appeared to the people of Wales when he turned out to play in my match against Hoovers in Merthyr Tydfil. They had never seen such a tall cricketer in the valleys. It was only when the morning mists cleared that his 6ft 5in cherubic countenance came into sight. They thought he was some second-row forward from the Cilfynydd Extra B until someone, taller than the average Welshman, caught sight of his coloured cap and blazer . . . red, pink and green . . . yes, the Heartaches . . . the amazing technicoloured heartaches.

Rice extravagated with the bat ('wandered from the right line into error' – *Oxford Abridged*) but he won the affection of the crowd by his extravisations of old English curse words every time he played and missed. The shot they liked best was the sudden surge forward of the superstar's left (front) leg to the pitch of the ball, accompanied by the slicing swish of the bat across to the right, a sort of knitting needle movement which brought gasps from the ignorant Welsh and a perfect caption from Max Boyce.

'Extra-bloody-ordinary shot that. How does he know the ball is always going to go over the top of the stumps?'

ERIC
MORECAMBE
The Double

SPORTSTHOUGHTS (OR A DAY WITH THE TAVERNERS)

I am better known as a comedian than a sportsman. People prove it constantly with expressions like 'That's Eric Morecambe – he's with Luton'. Morecambe and Luton . . . it has the ring of a cheap day return.

I have spent many happy minutes with Luton Town Football Club. I used to be a director of the club, but no longer. After six years, third division to first to second, I found that work and worry were becoming a little too much, so I gave up my directorship and now I'm vice-president, which means I get one free seat instead of four, and if we lose, much less aggravation! I still get invited to the directors' suite – and one of them is. Whatever happens I shall always follow 'my' team.

It's amazing how many people in show business want to be connected with sport in some way. Myself, it's Luton . . . Lord's Taverners . . . MCC . . . Goaldiggers . . . Sports Aid Foundation . . . I've appeared on *Pot Black*, at Wembley Cup Finals, and spent a whole afternoon with Dickie Davies on his *World of Sport*, and had numerous sporting dinners and luncheons, all most enjoyable. I've met the people who run the games and the people who are the games. I've had lunch with Ron Greenwood and the whole of the staff and players of the England team, and didn't have to work – just be there. I was given a complete England soccer outfit, except the boots . . . I take size seven on the left and nine on the right, and they wouldn't split a pair! I have a thousand memories, all because I was asked by a man called Tony Hunt, then Chairman of Luton, if I would join the board. And when I did, most of my friends thought I was mad. In the last ten years I have been involved with the most wonderful businesses in the world: show business and sport.

But I'm not the only entertainer to do this. Take Elton John – he'll go – affectionately known as the Watford Gap. He's sport-orientated (it's the way he walks). Pete Murray . . . he's the one who supports Arsenal. Well, the first four letters are right. How many people who have borrowed this book know that Marty Feldman is a tennis fanatic? He can actually go to Wimbledon and watch a game without moving his head . . . Ernie Wise, who once thought Billy Bremner was the Chancellor of West Germany . . . now Ernie follows Clydebank, Barclays Bank and Nat West Ham.

How many times have we watched the pro-am golf on television? Wonderful matches, with people like Gary Player and Lee Trevino playing little Olga Corbett of the Two Ronnies, and Sean Coronary. Is it generally known that Patrick Mower follows both Bristols, so that he can see the game home and away? Larry Grayson goes to Queens Park . . . Henry Cooper is a pugilist. (He doesn't know, he thinks he's a boxer.) Every morning Henry's wife has to count up to ten before he'll get up!

It's like the old saying 'Actors want to be comics, and comics want to be actors'. Well, it's the same with sport. Showbiz people want to be sportsmen and sportsmen want to be showpeople . . . Freddie Trueman is well known for his after dinner speaking. When he speaks he's usually after dinner. It's also a well-known fact that Rachael Heyhoe Flint knows more dirty jokes than Freddie . . . and that's saying something.

At the mention of Rachael, we seem to forget that sport is not all men. For sport you need women (well for the sport I play). Women play cricket, football, tennis – almost every game. And in my opinion they bring glamour into any sport. Look at the minute amount of clothes they wear . . . my grandmother went to bed in more clothes than Virginia Wade won Wimbledon in!

One of the best things that has happened to me in sport is being made the President of the Lord's Taverners, a charity organisation that was started through cricket, although now it has added golf and boxing to its Patrick Mower bosom.

The Lord's Taverners has a list of names from both sport and show business personalities, longer than Nelson's right arm. (It's hard to realise that he used to live with David Hamilton.) Mr Tim Brooke-Taylor – there's three for a start. John Alderton . . . what a fine actor that man is. In that wonderful series *Thomas and Sarah* he played Sarah . . . he couldn't play Thomas, not with a name like John. Willie Rushton, with his flaming red beard: the last time I saw anything like that on a face, the whole herd had to be destroyed! Another name comes to mind – Fiona Richmond. But that's got nothing to do with you! Tim Rice, co-author of such great hits as *Patrick Moore Super Star*, and *Ryvita* . . . anyone in showbiz who is anyone, is in the Taverners. And don't forget that behind every star is a surprised wife.

These stars give up their spare and precious time for us, so that we may give to under-privileged children, playing fields, coaches for the handicapped, and cricket facilities. This takes a lot of money, and a lot of money takes a lot of finding . . .

As I've already said, not everyone in the Taverners is in show business. There are many famous sportsmen and women. I mean, how's this for name dropping . . . The Nawab of Pataudi – eh? Be honest . . . how about that.

I remember once having a drink with his Sirocco . . . I was on neat gin and crisps and he was on Indian tonic and poppadums. As always, the conversation got round to cricket and I asked him a direct question about a certain English player. Now for at least half a minute he couldn't answer. He just looked at me with his face going slowly red and his eyes bulging . . . Evidently a piece of poppadum had slipped down the wrong way. I slapped his back and the offending object flew across the room and landed in the mynah bird's cage. The bird ate it and never spoke again. I repeated the question – 'What do you think of Bedser?' and Nawab said, 'I don't sleep on bed sir, I sleep on rush mat'. Nawab lives in New Delhi near India and next to Nicholas Parsons.

Of course, the Taverners have certain rules. Two that I can remember: one is Deaf O'Connor can never be a member, and the second is we do not allow political jokes because sometimes they get elected.

All our members wait eagerly for April, knowing that soon we will thrill to the sound of leather hitting Brian Close. Prince Charles was our last President, while at the moment I'm your last . . . (that doesn't sound quite right) . . . President.

Prince Philip (by the way he can verify the Nawab story – next time you see him, just ask). He's our Twelfth Man. That means if we are ever short we ring up the Palace and ask the Queen if he can come out and play. She's usually very good about letting him come with us on Sundays, except if he has to mow the lawn before one of the garden parties.

Freddie Trueman plays for us often as he can. Fred is known as a quickie, but nowadays that's usually after the game.

Every Sunday in the cricket season we play a team for charity, and the kindness and hospitality shown to us by our hosts is tremendous. Everyone enjoys themselves so much. Usually an enormous marquee is put up for our players and their friends, and their players and their friends. In this marquee we have lunch, tea and drinks – but not necessarily in that order. There are always lots of stars to be seen, both male and female, and let me tell you this, sunshine, if you're invited in to that marquee, your year is made. You will see, do and hear things your vicar wouldn't believe, or if you're Jewish, your priest . . .

You could bump into Geoff Boycott: to some people a genius, to others not a genius. To me it depends on how you define the word. A genius can be a nudist with a memory for faces . . . or Geoff Boycott.

You could bump into Barry Sheene, John Conteh, Reg Simpson, Bill Edrich or John Snow, even Denis Compton. And if you're lucky you could bump into Pauline Collins. (She plays Thomas in *George and Mildred*.) She may be there because John Alderton is there. Because they have been pronounced 'bed and breakfast'.

You might bump into Patrick Moore. Now he has a devastating googly, which in all probability has been caused by his run up . . . or the fact that he's put his cricket box on upside down. You might bump into Ronnie Barker or trip over Ronnie Corbett. You could share a joke with the Earl of Ranfurley, KCMA: eat a waiter with Donald Pleasance: have a drink with Colin Milburn: write a song with Michael Margolis, FRSA, MSTD, MADCC, MISA: pick a fight with Noel Gordon. All this can be done before you sit down to lunch or the game starts. And the food is home cooking, which is where a lot of men in the marquee think their wives are.

Imagine it's July, a boiling hot afternoon, ruined only by the pouring rain and the wind. You have been honoured . . . you are wearing a 'Taverners' name tab . . . this has your name on it. Also you will wear a name tab on one of your socks. (That's in case you end up under the table; you'll know who you are. If through having a few too many you lose the name tab on your jacket, make sure you take your sock with the other name tab on it off . . . otherwise only half of you is sent back home.)

But at the moment you are sober, and you keep your eyes on the tent flap as star after star weaves in. You are standing by the bar, at one end of the marquee. It's early yet, 11.45 to be exact. You've been standing in line for the last fifteen minutes waiting your turn to get a drink. 'A gin and tonic please' you beam, 'with ice', you grin. 'No ice' the lady who serves you grimaces. The thing to do then is not to say anything, but just let her look at your glass and you'll feel it go cold in your hand. If you are going to stay on gin and tonic, and you happen to be one of the lucky early ones that gets a piece of lemon, hold on to it. The same applies to the glass. Keep it with you at all times, even though when you hold it up to the sun you can't see the drink in it for your fingerprints! Watch out for your lemon . . . there have been more lemon slices stolen on these occasions than money.

You now walk away from the bar through the long grass underfoot. You have a drink, two name tabs, a piece of lemon, and a smell of the country coming from your shoes. You are now at liberty to talk or listen to anyone. The lemon in your drink is as good as being a mason. Suddenly the marquee flap opens and a man enters with an old cricket bag. You are taken back almost fifty years – a hero of your youth, and he was getting on a bit then. I'm not going to say how old this ex-England player is; it wouldn't be fair. Suffice it to say he was there when the great W.G. Grace said 'Son, I think I'll grow a beard'. And what he lacks in muscle he makes up for in flab. He heads straight for the bar.

You walk around the marquee, you hear snatches of conversations:

First actress: 'I must say, darling, I think your husband dresses nattily.'

Second actress: 'Natalie who?'

You move on . . .

First star's son: 'My father's better than yours.'

Second star's son: 'No he isn't.'

First star's son: 'And my brother's better than yours.'

Second star's son: 'No he isn't.'

First star's son: 'And my mother's better than yours.'

Second star's son: 'Well you could be right there because my father says that.'

A little further on . . .

Major: 'Well, I'll tell you this old fruit, I never had any er – you know – er, relationships with my wife before we were married. How about you, eh?'

Major Star: 'I don't know . . . what was your wife's maiden name?'

The place is beginning to fill. Lunch is in forty minutes, just about time to get another drink.

At the bar will be a group of people whom you have never seen on film, TV or colour radio. Unknown to you, these men will probably be the Lord's Taverners council. They may be having a debate . . . now a debate to them is something you catch fish with.

After lunch, the game starts. You, through having two name tabs and a piece of lemon, can go and stand in the enclosure, a roped-off area to stop people from touching or getting too near the stars. It will be packed, because the ropes are now on the ground. The man whose job it is to keep them up and stop the people from touching the stars is also their umpire. You may be fortunate to stand next to an ex-England cricket star and watch him be sick. Let me add this is not caused by drink. This is what, at some time or another, we all suffer from – nerves. Here is a man who has in his time stood up to Lindwall and Miller, Lillee and Thomson, Adelaide and Sydney, even Little and Large. But now in front of maybe fifty to sixty people he has to face Arthur Askey, who is 5 for 77. (That's his height and age.) I would advise you to go back into the marquee and watch a fight between the actor who got the part, and the one who thought he should have got it. Suddenly you hear the rapturous applause as Askey has claimed the sick ex-England star cricketer's wicket. The latter is now swaying back to the pavilion. The next man is due in . . . no . . . no, we've declared: 151 for 13.

You rush towards the tea urn. The woman serving looks directly at you. It's the same woman who served you the g and t. She hands you your tea: it's as cold as a mother-in-law's kiss.

One of our stars has been hurt. A cake has fallen on his foot. An ambulance man comes over to attend to it. He must be all of ninety-five . . . he couldn't put a dressing on a salad.

You hear scattered conversation.

Male: 'What's your husband getting for his birthday?'

Female: 'Bald and fat!'

Star: 'What's on this plate in case I have to describe it to a doctor?'

Female: 'If he'd really loved me he'd have married someone else . . . '

Today you have been part of the Lord's Taverners . . . you have mixed with stars, you have talked to beautiful women, you have contributed. It does not matter who wins the game as long as we do. It's getting towards dusk, it's going home time. A star gets into his chauffeur driven Rolls with a beautiful lady. The car won't start, the chauffeur lifts the bonnet, the star and the beautiful lady go back to the marquee . . . the Taverners' motto is being taken down – 'Sleep is best, next to a beautiful woman'.

One more drink and back to the Rolls. The chauffeur is still tinkering with the car. The beautiful woman speaks –

'Would you like a screwdriver?'

The chauffeur replies, 'You're very kind madam but I'd like to get the car started first'.

The perfect end to a perfect day.

MICHAEL
JAYSTON
Boundary

TRENT BRIDGE BUCCANEERS

Cricket has provided such a wealth of literature, from Dickens through Priestley, Pinter, Cardus and Arlott, that it is daunting for an amateur scribbler to know where to begin. As earliest memories burn vividly, I shall recount some of mine, from the time I was a cricket-besotted lad in Nottingham; I shall describe some of the heroes I encountered. In an age when heroes are in short supply, I use the word 'hero' unreservedly.

At the age of eleven my knowledge of the game was encyclopaedic and my love for it boundless. However, in the middle of that particular season I was led astray by a nine-year-old beauty called Rosemary, and by some fellow urchins who, like me, were courting her. Thinking to impress her we got up to numerous pranks, one of which was to drop lumps of ice-lolly from the Trent Bridge stand down the dresses of the ladies beneath.

It was for Rosemary that I stole some geraniums that grew in window boxes in front of the pavilion at Trent Bridge and which were the pride and joy of Colonel H.A. Brown, then secretary of Notts CC. I was caught and hauled before him. He was a kindly man, but warned me that if I was caught again I would be banned from watching the next home match at the ground.

At that moment I saw Rosemary in her true light. She was spotty, wouldn't let me hold her hand, didn't like my gifts of geraniums and, much worse, I had a sneaking suspicion she knew nothing about cricket! I renounced her there and then.

About three weeks later I was sipping a Dandelion and Burdock in a sweet shop just outside Trent Bridge when I saw an elderly gentleman slip and fall into the gutter. I helped him to his feet and then across the road. He thanked me, 'Here lad, buy yourself an ice-cream', he said and gave me sixpence, which bought three ice-creams in those days. As he gave me the coin I suddenly realised who he was.

'You're George Gunn', I blurted out.

'Now, how the devil do you know that, you could never have seen me play' he said.

It was indeed the legendary George Gunn: the man who, while recuperating from TB in Australia in 1912, had replaced an injured batsman and scored a century on his Test debut: the man who had told the fearsome Australian fast bowler, MacDonald, that he couldn't knock the skin off a rice pudding and when MacDonald bowled a bumper next ball, hit him for six over third man! George seemed modestly pleased that I knew so much about him. After that first meeting I saw him from time to time and he always had a smile and a cheery wave of his stick for me.

September came, and with it the last match of the season. After the game was over I walked round the ground. I had my cricket bag with me because of a game that morning. The nets at Trent Bridge for some reason were still up and who should be there but George Gunn.

'Hello young fellow me lad. You won't have much more chance of games this year', he said, with reference to my equipment. 'Have you got a cricket ball in your bag?'

I said I had.

'Come on, you can turn your arm over and we'll see how good you are.'

For the next twenty minutes or so I bowled to George Gunn, who played with his walking stick. In that time he missed just one ball, whereupon he picked up a stump.

'This is a bit better', he said. 'My eyes aren't what they used to be.' He was then over seventy years of age.

After about half an hour of bowling I was tiring, but he appeared to want to carry on until it was dark. Then he said 'I scored nearly eight hundred runs in one innings on this part of the ground'.

I must have looked disbelieving because he then told me a story which I have since verified. In 1919 George was at the head of the national averages. A local amateur cricketer of meagre ability had the audacity to challenge George to a single wicket competition for a £100 side wager; a considerable amount in those days. George, not being a greedy man and knowing that the game would be completely one-sided, refused the invitation. The amateur persisted and badgered George for weeks. At last George, out of sheer exasperation, agreed, reducing the wager to a fiver, but determined to teach the fellow a lesson. The match was played on the Trent Bridge practice ground from five until seven-thirty in the evening. George won the toss and batted. At the end of the first evening he had scored exactly 300 not out. By the end of the second session he was 620 not out. At which point the amateur suggested that George might like to declare. George declined, saying he never declared in a single wicket match, but adding that the amateur could substitute the stumps for a heavy roller which was six feet wide! It made not the slightest difference. Halfway through the third evening George had increased his score to 777, and had just run nine off one hit when the amateur finally cracked.

Perhaps the realisation that he could possibly be bowling to George throughout the winter eventually decided the issue in his mind. Conceding the match, he threw the ball down and stomped off to the *Trent Bridge Inn*, from where he was seen emerging three hours later in a deplorable and maudlin condition.

'And what was worse', said George, concluding the story, 'after all that palaver he never paid me the fiver we'd wagered. Still, one good thing came out of it. I had so much practice from him that I think he had something to do with my being top of the national averages that year. I hope I didn't ruin his enjoyment of the game', he said, with a wicked twinkle in his eye.

The following season, 1947, I was to witness performances by a Notts batsman that I have still to see bettered in their sheer elegance of achievement. Whenever the name Joe Hardstaff is mentioned to cricketers of his generation the word 'classic' is always used. In the year of the 'Middlesex Twins', Hardstaff conjured his own particular brand of magic. I saw him score 200 not out against Somerset, 127 not out against Glamorgan, and 221 and 45 both not out against Warwickshire! Towards the end of the season he scored 545, for once out, which I believe is still a record in England. Joe had every stroke in the book; a majestic cover drive, a delicate leg glance, and a stroke you hardly see nowadays, the late cut, which when executed by Joe usually bisected slips and gully, leaving third man racing desperately to try to stop a boundary. During that year and the two following, Hardstaff continued to amass large scores and finished in 1949 top of the averages. Yet, inexplicably, he played for England only once in that period, although he had played many times before. Perhaps his omission was due to the fact that he had been rude to the wife of one of the selectors. Perhaps, as was often darkly murmured by the Notts members, it was because you have to play that much better if you do not belong to one of the more 'fashionable' clubs. The one Test he played was against the all conquering Australians of 1948, and in the first innings, amazingly, he was caught by Keith Miller in the slips for 0.

My idol was out, and if Miller that day could have been struck dead by mental telepathy it would have saved England a lot of trouble in the years to come! I consoled myself with the fact that Miller was a great cricketer, and that no one else on the field could have made the catch. Joe did score a splendid 43 in the second innings when England had their backs to the wall, and Compton made 184.

Hardstaff wasn't picked again for his country but continued to score in a prolific manner for Notts. Joe's partner in many an exciting finish was Reg Simpson, a brilliant stroke maker in his own right and soon to be an inspiring and adventurous captain for his country. I wish aspiring young cricketers of today could have seen those two. When they were 'on song', no field could be set to contain them. Their hitting, when quick runs were needed, was not the indiscriminate slogging one sometimes sees in limited overs cricket. It was brilliant, controlled, powerful stroke play. As examples, I mention four matches in 1949 to illustrate not only their achievements but that of the Notts team as a whole. Against Northants they scored 245 in 145 minutes to win the match. Hardstaff scored a century in each innings. Against Surrey, in an attack which included Bedser and Laker, Notts scored 209 in 97 minutes to win. Simpson scored a not out double century in the first innings. Against Hampshire they again won by knocking up 226 in 113 minutes. The most remarkable feat in a remarkable month was the match against Leicester when, set to score 279 in 145 minutes, they actually hit off the runs in 107 minutes – or 156 an hour! They scored off every one of the 35 overs bowled, which in terms of today's limited overs cricket is just one run under eight an over! Simpson, not to be outdone by Hardstaff, scored a century in each innings of the Leicester game. The figure boldly stated cannot capture the manner and style with which the runs were made – the gauntlet thrown down and accepted, the nail-biting tension. This happened, too, in an age many cricket writers said was a 'play safe' era. I wish they would 'play safe' like that today.

The other favourite memory I have of that time was about two years later. Notts were badly depleted by injury and illness. The Notts coach, Bill Voce, who had not played for some time, was pressed into service against Sussex. His days of glory as Harwood's partner were long since over and at the age of forty-two, short of match practice, little could have been expected of him. In the event, he rolled back the years, bowled 33 overs and took 5 Sussex wickets including those of John Langridge and David Sheppard, the two openers. This alone would have satisfied most ordinary men, but there was more to come. Voce came in when Notts were in some trouble after losing 5 wickets, and hit 45 runs including two colossal sixes over the ladies' pavilion. The ball which caused his dismissal flicked off the edge of his bat on to his nose, and was then caught by the wicket-keeper. He walked from the wicket, blood pouring down his face, like a triumphant gladiator, and fifty yards from the pavilion the members rose as one man to applaud the warrior.

Years later I met him when he came to work at the Bestwood Colliery offices, and spent many happy times chatting with him when I should have been working as an aspiring cost accountant. He played for the Bestwood side for one season and I played against him for Gedling Colliery. By now Bill had reverted to his original slow left arm spinners. I had scored about 20 runs when Bill came on and I hit his first ball for four! He glared down the wicket at me with beetle brows. The next ball was certainly not slow. It whipped through, short of a length and hit me painfully in the lower ribs. It was as if Bill was saying 'Don't forget I bowled at Bradman'. The next ball bowled me neck and crop. As I was walking out I heard Bill say 'I think I've found a length now'. Youth is certainly no substitute for experience.

Trent Bridge today still evokes the memories of those golden days. It must have rained at some time but I can only remember the sunshine, the moustached colonels (retired) in the members' enclosure, and George Parr's tree. Mention must be made of this last edifice. George Parr, the Lion of the North, circa 1845, used to hit balls to leg into the branches of an oak which was situated some ninety yards from the wicket. He did it so often that the tree was named after him. Sadly it was destroyed in a gale three years ago. Many slivers of it now reside on mantelpieces. I believe Leslie Crowther, who was staying in a hotel nearby at the time, even has a branch!

It was George Parr who gave this sound advice to young cricketers of his day.

'When you play in a match, be sure not to forget to pay a little attention to the umpire. First of all enquire after his health, then say what a fine player his father was, and finally, present him with a brace of birds or rabbits. This will give you confidence and you will probably do well.'

With the amount of matches the modern day cricketer has to play, he would be hard pressed financially to accommodate all the umpires, unless of course he did a spot of poaching in his spare time.

My obvious bias towards Nottinghamshire Cricket Club and its players stems from the fact that I first learned my love of the game at Trent Bridge. Of course I saw many wonderful players from other counties, whom I grudgingly accepted were the equals of and in some cases better than 'my team'. Since joining the Lord's Taverners I have appeared on the same field as some of them in charity matches: Trueman, Cowdrey, Barrington, Evans, Compton, Graveney, Bailey, Bill Edrich, Laker, Reg Simpson – there's a roll of honour for you. I possess a much thumbed score card which bears the legend: 'D.C.S. Compton bowled Jayston 10'. I mention this certainly not to brag about the achievement, but to illustrate the measure of Compton in particular and cricketers in general. The great man had come in, and with his celebrated leg sweep had scored a couple of boundaries. The next ball I bowled turned a few inches. Compton once more went to sweep and the ball hit his wicket. *Sotto voce* I hissed to the umpire 'call a no ball'. After all it was a charity match and the crowd had come to see Compton, not me. The umpire was in the process of lifting his arm, but Compton was on his way to the pavilion, waving his bat in acknowledgement.

After the match I sought him out in the bar, and falteringly started to say I wasn't trying to make a name for myself and that I could have bowled another thousand balls and not got him out. He stopped my ramblings short, saying 'Don't be silly, good ball, bad stroke. I've bought you a large gin'. When I said I was sorry, I never touched gin, he said 'Never mind, I'll drink that, have a pint'. This kind of humility and generosity I have found in so many cricketers of his generation. In charity games they listen patiently to actors and 'celebrities' recounting their own petty exploits and give them encouragement and advice. I agree entirely with Cardus when he wrote 'Cricketers ought never to know of old age. Every springtime ought to find them newborn, like the green world they live in.'

All the cricketers I have ever met, from George Gunn onwards, and whose deeds sprinkle *Wisden*, have one thing in common, which I can only explain by a quotation from the Grand Old Man himself. W.G. Grace had met an old player who had been a famous cricketer of his own day, and Grace said of him:

'My star was in the ascendant, his had long since declined, but he still had the light of battle on his face, and I could see what manner of man he had been.'

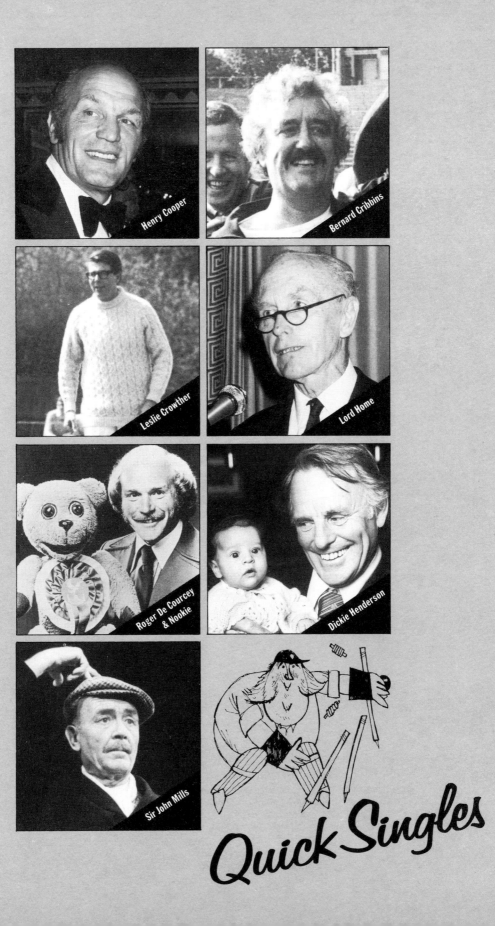

Henry Cooper

Bernard Cribbins

Leslie Crowther

Lord Home

Roger De Courcey & Nookie

Dickie Henderson

Sir John Mills

Quick Singles

HENRY COOPER *Slogger*

FOLLOW THAT!

A few years ago, I was invited to appear on a television show with the good Dr Edith Summerskill, who was very anti-boxing. The show had been going on for about ten minutes, when out of the blue – in a very superior voice – she said:

'Mr Cooper, have you looked in a mirror and seen the state of your nose?'

Well, I thought to myself, I must come back at you luv, so I said:

'Madam, have you looked in a mirror lately and seen the state of *your* nose? Boxing was my excuse, what's yours?'

BERNARD CRIBBINS *Bye*

BYE (BYE BYE)

My most embarrassing moment in cricket happened in my very first game. I was introduced to the Taverners by the late Sid James and Peter Haigh. The game was on the county cricket ground at Hove, and the teams were the usual mixture of actors, cricketers, and odds and sods. I found the whole thing somewhat bewildering as I'd *never* played proper cricket before. (At school in Oldham we played with the wicket chalked on the wall, and a tennis ball and a plank. I don't remember ever appearing in a proper game.)

Our side was in the field, and I did the running about near the boundary collecting the ball from spectators after every four or six, and chucking it back to the bowler. Then came the great moment. Sid James came up and said that I was the next bowler at the other end and what sort of a field setting did I want. I said 'whatever you think best Sid', and he gave me a very funny look. Anyway, the over finished, and I was given the ball. I chatted with the umpire about what I was bowling, and after the first ball he called it 'right arm rubbish'.

Anyway, I took what I thought was enough of a run and hurled the ball down the leg side and was hit for four. This happened with the next ball too. Then our opponents took a single, and I was facing a very tough, determined looking batsman. I added a couple of yards to my run and belted one at him. Whack! Another four. But the next ball did the trick. He stepped forward to hammer it over my head and his off stump had gone. I couldn't believe it. My first wicket in a *proper game*. I was leaping about shouting 'Owzat', and all the other things that successful bowlers shout, when Sid strolled over, gave me the ball and said 'Calm down will you, he's an ice hockey player . . .'

LESLIE CROWTHER *Leg Before*

Leslie Crowther writes: 'A few years ago I visited a Boys' Club in Sneinton Dale. The lads there were taking part in a marathon charity vault in aid of the local branch of the Spastics Society. I was moved to write the following lines.'

SNEINTON DALE

There is a Boys' Club down in Sneinton Dale,
Where strength and fellowship go hand in hand,
Where on a Sunday morning gathered there
Proud parents sitting round on bentwood chairs,
Their wiry children leaping over vaults,
A Sponsored Marathon for Charity.

The crippled folk for whom they took the air
Are only able in their dreams to emulate
The acrobatic curves and soaring flight
Denied to them by a misshapen birth;
Unable to control unwilling limbs,
Unwilling to accept their uncontrol.

The courage of the spastic is well known,
Encouraged by so many helping hands
Who help them so to bear their twisted fate
And strive so hard to lead a normal life
That they acquire a sense of humour rare
And seem to wear an ever present smile.

That smile would widen if they could but see
The efforts of those boys who strove so hard
To earn the money guaranteed by friends.
I only hope those children realise
How moving were the movements they performed
That Sunday morning down in Sneinton Dale.

Quick Singles

LORD HOME OF THE HIRSEL *Not Out*

PRAYER OF A CRICKETER'S WIFE

'Oh God, if there is to be cricket
in heaven let there also be rain.'

ROGER DE COURCEY AND NOOKIE BEAR *A Pair*

A PAIR

What is to be said about a 'pair'? In cricketing terms, there is not too much to hope for – except, of course, you can't get any worse the next time. For us – Nookie and I – a 'pair' means the two of us working in harmony, with the goal of the public's satisfaction in mind.

Nookie's cricketing experience is limited, to the extent of paranoia! As a bear, he spends most of the winter in hibernation. He wakes in the spring, to look forward to the cricketing summer ahead. Thus he enjoys the ultimate perfection that a lot of Taverners must strive for – sleeping all winter, missing all and every football match, and being fully awake only during the cricket season!

His partner, however, having been born in Vauxhall, within a boundary's distance of The Oval, started his cricketing career under the guidance of Arthur McIntyre as a wicket keeper. He made such an impact that he's now a ventriloquist! Casting my mind back to those days, remembering the Colts and ground staff, the 'pair' who stick in my mind were two real cricketing characters – which these days seem to be in somewhat short supply. These two were 'Dapper Constable' and fifty-or-nothing Arthur McIntyre! I can't remember exactly how many times I saw Constable run for a ball and lose his hat – but it seems countless.

May Nookie and I wish all the Taverners a very successful time on the green, for this year and in the future.

DICKIE HENDERSON *A Big Hit*

A SOBERING THOUGHT

Ken Barrington, while sitting at lunch with Harry Secombe, Max Bygraves, Eric Sykes, and myself, cracked one of the best gags we'd ever heard. None of us tried to top it.

He had retired from first-class cricket with a heart condition, and after several years of married life, his wife presented him with his first child.

The usual time-worn remarks came from the assembled group of professional comedians. Ken came out with the immortal tag line:

'The reason it has taken so long is because I played so many long innings for England that I forgot to take the box off.'

SIR JOHN MILLS *Half Century*

A CASE OF MISTAKEN IDENTITY

Here is a short anecdote – something that happened to me in Australia. Actually, it was after Australia, in Penang. I had been doing a promotional whizz-round of Brisbane, Adelaide, Perth, Melbourne and Sydney, all in seven days. We had a terrific time, and were given the full treatment – large black limousine at the foot of the aircraft, and so on.

We then took off for Penang for a week's rest. The first evening we arrived, there was a barbecue on the beach. I spotted one lady glancing at me from time to time, and I was just reaching for my pen to sign her menu when she leaned across, and, in a loud, clear voice, said:

'Excuse me, but aren't you Bobby Howes?'

I said, 'No, Madam, and I am very relieved to say that I am not, because Bobby Howes passed away about ten years ago . . .'!

Quick Singles

RAYMOND BAXTER
Off Drive

OFF DRIVE

Probably the most off drive I ever experienced was in the Monte Carlo Rally of, I believe, 1958. That it should have been so was particularly sad, because the event marked my one and only appearance in international competition as a works driver for Aston Martin. Reg Parnell drove one of the other team cars I remember – and also made a pig's ear of the event – while the third car was driven by Eric Thompson, who used to take time off from Lloyds to win prizes in all sorts of places from Spa to Le Mans. Since, in those days, I still had an office in Broadcasting House – shared, I may add, with Brian Johnston – it was a clear case of the BBC motoring above its station. So it probably served me right. Not that we didn't try: in fact, on reflection, 'trying' was the operative word for the entire affair.

Despite what you may hear to the contrary from the younger generation, the Monte Carlo Rally was in those days, as now, very hard work. That is, if you took the event seriously. By 'seriously', I mean that you tried to win something, as opposed to just getting there in order to look up old friends in Rosey's Bar. Of course, getting to Rosey's Bar was the primary target for all my friends anyway, from Paddy Hopkirk to Graham Hill – but you take my point.

Anyway, the year in question (and the fourteen consecutive years in which I did lunatic things to get to Rosey's Bar tend to merge into a happy nostalgic blur) was particularly hard. That is to say it snowed even before we got to Glasgow.

Now before I am accused by the Twelfth Man of *lèse-majesté* for inappropriate use of the first person plural, may I hastily explain that rally drivers, like Lord's Taverners, tend to use 'we' when referring to their exploits. It takes at least two persons to make a rally car complete, as in so many of the more enjoyable human activities.

On this occasion my partner was one Jackie Reece. In addition to being one of my closest friends, Jackie was also a very successful driver in the days when motorsport was rather more than an arrangement for providing the fastest mobile advertising hoardings yet devised. Not only that, he was, and still is, one of the best raconteurs I have ever met. When I tell you that he also has a stutter matched only by Patrick Campbell in full cry, you will realise that he was the ideal companion with whom to be cooped up in a car for four days and three nights en route to Rosey's – always assuming that one's purpose was also to collect some silverware from Prince Rainier at the conclusion of the event.

My first encounter with Jackie was prior to the start of the 1951 Rally. He was sharing a Ford Popular with his equally amazing cousin, Peter. As Jackie tinkered with the engine outside the Royal Scottish Automobile Club in Blythswood Square, Glasgow, I asked him, 'live' microphone in hand, if the lack of a rev counter did not present problems when coaxing the last ounce of power on the passes of the Maritime Alps.

'Certainly not' he replied. 'When the k-knob on the end of the g-gear lever g-glows cherry-red I ch-change up.'

So it was that some seven years later, as dusk deepened towards the third night of the rally, we found ourselves descending the pass that led to the bridge at Castellane. By this time there were few competitors still in the hunt across the endless miles of snow and ice. The Aston was running like a bird. Jackie was driving.

The gradient was perhaps one in fourteen down; the surface was polished, rutted ice. Studded tyres had yet to be invented – but that is another story. The road was a typical 'D' route in the mountains, consisting of short straights between successive hairpins. We were travelling at around sixty mph, and I was making time and distance calculations against the next control.

'Does the master require anything?' I asked.

'Of course', said Jackie, 'but we didn't b-bring it with us'.

'Apart from that', I said. 'A drink of orange juice perhaps?'

'Excellent', he said, 'provided that the v-vintage can be relied upon'.

I knelt in my seat and rummaged around in the back of the Aston for an unfrozen can. Came a discreet tap on my ankle.

'T-turn round and f-face the front', he said.

I turned, and there, fifty yards in front of us, was the biggest *camion* in France with a trailer in tow, slithering slowly up towards us from the next hairpin, and occupying the entire road. To the right, there was three thousand feet of Alp straight up; to the left, an eight hundred foot drop to the village of Castellane.

'I j-just wanted you', said my co-driver, 'to have a g-good view of this accident'.

At the risk of spoiling the story, I have in fairness to record that we hit neither *camion* nor trailer – nor even the high banks of snow which lined the road. We ran out of 'electrics' a hundred and fifty miles further on, but that, too, is another story.

JOHN
SNAGGE
Top Scorer

THE RIDE OF MY LIFE

Ever since I can remember I have always had an ambition to ride on a fire engine, on a genuine call for help. It has taken me until the age of seventy-five to achieve that ambition, and it happened by accident – as indeed do most fires.

I was due to record a programme for BBC radio about the work of the London Fire Brigade. The venue was to be Shaftesbury Avenue, a branch station. We duly arrived – the producer, Roger Clarke, the recording engineer, Graham Clifford, and myself – with the willing consent of the sub officer in charge. He had agreed to sound the station alarm bell, so that the duty firemen would come sliding down the pole. Then orders would be given, the engines of the vehicles started up, and the doors clang open. All this was to be staged purely for sound effects.

Everything went according to plan, and was splendidly acted out by all concerned. With that recording on the tape, I could start my interviews and descriptions of the firemen's jobs and the accompanying problems. We had just started this process when a true and genuine call came through. We thought 'that is the end of that'; we will have to try again some other time. But to our surprise the sub officer asked whether we would like to go with them. Needless to say, we answered 'yes, most certainly', and climbed aboard the fire engine, the recording engineer clutching his tape machine.

Blue lamps flashed, sirens kept up a steady wail, and bells were clanged from time to time. But where, we wondered, were we going? Having manoeuvred through Shaftesbury Avenue to Piccadilly Circus, we rounded the corner into Regent Street. I whispered to my colleagues, 'Could it be Broadcasting House?'! We got within sight of the building but then we learned the call had come from St George's Hotel. In fact, though it was not a hoax, there was no fire either. It appeared that an automatic fire alarm had set itself off, so our attendance was not required, and we went back to base – this time under quite normal conditions, without blue lights, bells or sirens. We took the normal course of an ordinary vehicle.

But that first emergency drive was something I shall never forget. The fireman driver was brilliant. The behaviour of the traffic – buses, taxis, vans and ordinary cars – was exemplary. Way was made as far as was humanly possible at red lights: everyone halted and allowed us through. I suppose a normal journey such as the one we made would have taken nearly half an hour: by the courtesy of all the other drivers, we got to our destination in just about seven minutes. I learned later that the only privilege for fire engines is the right to exceed the speed limit. Accidents which might occur, such as when crossing traffic lights that are red, being on the wrong side of islands, and ignoring other traffic regulations, are the firemen's responsibility. They are liable for any such accident. Our fireman driver was truly superb. It seemed to me that sometimes he avoided other road users by mere inches. If only everyone could drive with that sort of skill, there would be few accidents anywhere.

However, this was not the only incident that took place. After we had returned to the branch station, we took up once more the recording we had come to do. Then I was asked if I was prepared to go up the turn-table ladder with my microphone and tell my story as I saw the surrounding area from a height of some eighty feet or so. Now I had done this once before in 1939, but thought I would do it again in spite of all the years in between. It was pouring with rain but that was of no importance. I was duly dressed in the proper equipment – a heavy oilskin coat, a helmet (most comfortable) and a four-inch leather belt with a hook clamp attached. I climbed the ladder's first stage, some twenty-five rungs, safely guarded by a fireman. When I reached the top of this first extension, I had been instructed to hold out my hand to indicate that all was well. Then the other sections would be raised as and when I was ready.

With microphone poised, I waited a few minutes for my guide and mentor to return to *terra firma*. Firmly clipped on to the ladder, I then raised my hand. The only response I had came through the loudspeaker which was their own ground communication:

'Sorry, you've got to come down. We've got a genuine call.'

I had just launched myself into a description of the Shaftesbury Avenue scene, and the Palace Theatre. But all that ended rather abruptly, and I had to clamber down, somewhat ignominiously, and be stripped of all my fireman's equipment.

To my sorrow, I never did get my free ride on the turn-table ladder, but I did at least fulfil the great childhood fantasy of riding a fire engine on a genuine call.

I add only that in talking to and spending some few hours in the company of the men who do the fireman's job, I have seldom been more impressed. They have such a sincere knowledge of their responsibilities, and above all such courage, such a strong belief in saving life, saving buildings, and protecting both – whatever the cost to themselves.

A postscript: It happens, as most people can see, that at my age I wear a hearing aid. In the hurry of descending the ladder, it became detached and I couldn't find it anywhere. However, on the return of the fire engine, the missing aid was found still aboard the craft, following its attendance at a genuine fire in Soho!

ROD
HULL & EMU
Silly Point

HIGHLIGHTS OF THE YEAR'S TELEVISION VIEWING

The *best* of 1980s television programmes especially selected for your enjoyment by Emu – Managing Director of Emu's Broadcasting Company, EBC1.

MARCH:

A great month for gardeners, and in this International Year of the Artichoke, our popular programme . . . *Radishes of yesterday* (repeat)

MAY:

And what a feast for sportsmen!

The result of the game between a soccer team from *Bryant and May* and one from *Swan Vestas* can be seen on *Match of the Day*.

CRICKET

Viewers will no doubt be entertained again by the play of the Lord's Taverners Twelfth Man – the one that fields the boundary on horseback and whacks the ball with a mallet.

ELECTION 1980

Following the vote of no confidence in the government, we shall be bringing you a *dramatised* version of the election entitled, *When the vote comes in.*

Again this will be seen in some regions as 'When the Rot Sets In' and in the Scottish Highlands as 'When the Goat Comes In'.

SEPTEMBER:

Famous Men of History This month's Famous Man is Sir Cecil Rhodes and deals with that period of his life when he was an 'angry young man'. Don't miss *Cross-Rhodes*.

Economics within the Government. 'How I Repaired my own Bicycle Wheel' by a government spokesman.

CHRISTMAS:

And *less films* will be shown this year than ever before. This follows complaints last year by many Irish viewers, who were so incensed by some of the films seen in their own homes that they slashed the seats. However the battle for the viewer still goes on and viewers will have a choice of seeing *Eric and Ernie* on one side, or by switching over will be able to see *Eric and Ernie.*

And that's it for this year, EMU

CLOSEDOWN POEM

I like to watch that 'Knockout' game.
I think the teams are daring.
But I can't stand that Stuart Hall
And isn't Eddie Waring?

I think it would be better
To have someone like Frank Bough.
Then I could watch the 'Knockout' game
Without the sound turned off.

SIR DONALD
BRADMAN
Century

RECIPE FOR DEVILLED STEAK

Sir Donald says: 'Here is my favourite recipe. You ought to cook yourself a steak from it and then you will realise how good it is'!

INGREDIENTS

2 tablespoons sugar
1 dessert spoon dark jam
2 tablespoons tomato sauce
1 large dessert spoon Worcester sauce
2 tablespoons vinegar
   pinch of salt

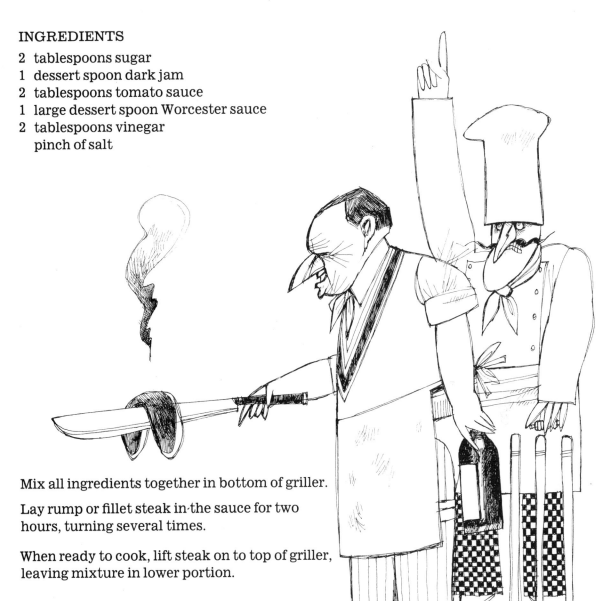

Mix all ingredients together in bottom of griller.

Lay rump or fillet steak in the sauce for two hours, turning several times.

When ready to cook, lift steak on to top of griller, leaving mixture in lower portion.

Grill for ten minutes.

Serve lower juice as gravy.

JAMES HUNT

Fastest Hundred

What the wicket-keeper saw . . .

ROBERT
POWELL
Hat-Trick

'CHARITY' CRICKET?

One of my most embarrassing moments on the cricket field took place when I was playing for the Vic Lewis XI against Surrey at The Oval. We were playing a ringer in our side, and I found myself going in to bat at number four, with no less than Rohan Kanhai at the other end. Between us we put on a Vic Lewis record for that wicket of over 100. Although this may sound like a marvellous performance from yours truly, in fact by the end of forty-five minutes I had scored approximately 26 and Kanhai had done the rest! He was magical to watch and I was struck almost completely immobile at times with amazement at his skill. Nevertheless I was fairly proud of my own contribution as the bowler was Intikhab Alam – one of the greatest spinners in the game. I played him gently with great caution and humility, which enabled me to push my score up to 26; as I have said, Kanhai did all the donkey work.

At the end of my forty-five minute innings, I strolled back to the pavilion, expecting to be met with applause and approbation from the other members of the team. Imagine the hurt and disappointment when, far from being impressed, they appeared to be agog with indifference. I ventured to enquire why no back slapping, no congratulations, no champagne, no accolades. It wasn't long before someone let slip the information that whenever Inti had been bowling to me, he had switched the ball and bowled *left handed*! In my 'hour of glory' I hadn't even noticed! Needless to say this revelation diminished my euphoria somewhat . . .

I did have my revenge a few weeks later when I was again playing for the Vic Lewis XI, this time against Surrey in Swindon. I caught Inti after he had only scored one run – as it happens totally by accident. I saw the ball speeding in my direction, imagined that I had absolutely no chance of stopping it, but in my enthusiasm stuck my hand out anyway. For some reason best known to itself the ball lodged there and Inti was out. It was all a mistake.

Somehow things never seem to work as you expect them to on the cricket field. I remember another incident at Edgbaston when Vic Lewis's XI (including Powell, R.) were playing against Warwickshire. Jameson opened the batting for Warwickshire and I opened the bowling. After seven overs, my figures were 0 for about 60. Slight depression set in. I asked Vic if I could be taken off, but he said that I should bowl just one more over.

Right, I thought. I bowled a couple of balls, revving myself up for a final fling. The next ball contained twenty years of suppressed violence and pent up cricket frustration – it was probably one of the best balls *ever* bowled. It swung like a banana, and was plumb on his middle stump – in fact, it had everything going for it.

Jameson hit it for six.

I fell to the ground in abject and total despair, and started to sob out my woes on the green sward. Jameson came over, and gently picked me up off the ground.

'I am so sorry', he said. 'That really was a great ball, and if it had been bowled to me in county cricket there is no way that I could have hit it like that. But I am afraid I had already decided to hit it for six before the ball even left your hand!'

Playing charity cricket with the pros certainly has its moments. When I played against Surrey I can remember that every time Graham Roope came in to bat, when he had hit 30 or 35 he would give me a nod and I would get a catch. Yorker, long hop, full toss, leg or off-break, it didn't matter: regardless of where I was fielding, and it was usually about a hundred yards away from him, I would get the ball straight into my hands without even having to move my feet.

I can remember another occasion when John Edrich complained because I was slowing the game down – by bowling on a length! That is the best notice I have ever had, either as an actor or as a cricketer.

Charity cricket has its gentlemen too. Playing against Kent one day at Blackheath, I was bowling to Colin Cowdrey. He strolled calmly down the wicket towards me, patting it down as he went. Without looking up, he said quietly: 'Just bowl one straight down the wicket.'

I did as he said, and almost before I knew it the off stump was gone: he had deliberately missed the ball by about three inches! He played the moment to the full, looking up at the crowd with a gesture of complete despair as if to say 'Wow! That one really beat me!' What a terrific bloke – to allow a rabbit like me to bowl him. Not all the younger players would allow that to happen. Far too much pride!

I remember one match in which I was playing with Julian Holloway and Michael Parkinson. During tea, Parky paused between mouthfuls of scone, thought for a moment, and then with great weight and deliberation accused Julian and myself of being the two most aggressive bastards he had ever seen on a cricket field! That sums it up really – all the actors, writers, and performers who get involved every Sunday in 'charity' cricket take the game very much to heart. In sitting-rooms from Hampstead to Barnes, when Boycott and Brearley go in to bat television sets are regaled with shouts of 'There, but for the grace of God, go I'!

NICHOLAS
PARSONS

The Umpire

THE UMPIRE

To misquote Sir Henry John Newbolt:

A breathless hush over Brian Close tonight,
Ten to make and the match to win,
A bumping pitch and a blinding light,
An hour to play and the last man in.

The tension is unbearable. Even the most dozey spectator has inched to the edge of his deck-chair, put aside his beer and sandwich, moved the newspaper from his head and the scorecard he was using as a book mark, and turned an eye to the game. Now he watches every move, knowing any action or lack of concentration by any player can determine the result of the match.

At these most crucial moments, there is one figure on the field of play whose responsibility becomes more and more awesome, and his position more and more isolated. A lone figure, owing no allegiance to any group or body, a man whose main attributes are experience, wisdom, and a white coat . . . The Umpire.

How does he feel, this paragon of impartiality, this symbol of all that is fair, square and above board, who has at all times to exercise his fullest concentration . . . and now even more so as he senses the drama of the situation? Behind his back, the bowler is pounding down the turf towards him; he mustn't flinch or turn away. The bowler is beside him; he whips the ball down the pitch; was that the third one in the over? Did he overstep the crease? Must he shout 'no ball'? The ball has hit the batsman's pad. Did it touch the bat first? If not, was it going to hit the stumps? As these thoughts rush through his mind in quick succession, the bowler turns and roars a deafening 'HOWZAT' straight into his face. This same intimidating cry is taken up by other fielders, and echoed by some of the crowd. There is a pause . . . a deathly hush. Now there is no escape, he must make a *decision*.

The chairman (or umpire) in a quiz show can, in the last resort, refer to what is written on his card; but out there on the sweaty green, all the umpire has between him and a public lynching is the vain hope that truth is all relative anyway. After all, much more is at stake here than a free holiday for two in Majorca.

So there he stands, a pounding heart concealed by a passive exterior, the result of the game hanging on whether in a few seconds he raises his finger in the air, or shakes his head. In those few seconds, he suddenly becomes aware that he is surrounded, not only by eleven aggressive cricketers, but by thousands of partisan and potentially threatening spectators – thousands . . . hundreds of thousands . . . millions even, if the match is being televised. As the tension of the moment gets to him, and it all starts going black, he hears a little voice within him repeating the end of Newbolt's verse,

'Play up! play up! and play the game'

and he wonders why he didn't choose an easier job!!

This brings to mind an old story, which to me illustrates very well the responsibilities and pressures that an umpire must face. It is a story about a man who goes to consult a psychiatrist because he feels he is on the edge of a nervous breakdown, and he blames the whole situation on the work that he does. The psychiatrist asks him to explain this, so the man says that he works at the fruit market and his job is to sort out the potatoes there. He has to grade them all for size; and this is what he does all day long. The psychiatrist remarks that he cannot see anything particularly arduous in that, at which the man gets very excited and says:

'Don't you see, doctor, all day I have to sort out these potatoes, and grade them into sizes. I have to put them into the large group, or the middle to large group, or the middle to small group, or the small group.'

So the psychiatrist says, 'I still don't see why this should be giving you a nervous breakdown.'

To which the man replies, 'Don't you see, doctor, all the time it's decisions, decisions, decisions!'

MICHAEL ASPEL

Scorer

SCORING

How ironic that one who has in his time excelled in gymnastics, rowing, tennis, swimming, rugby, boxing, sky-diving, hockey, pole-vaulting, Jokari, snooker and cricket should be relegated in this welter of reminiscences to the position of scorer.

I am prepared to compromise on the 'excelled' bit. I have certainly had a go at all the above activities. It may come as a surprise to those who have observed the undeviating straightness of my nose that during my National Service I was asked to represent my battalion as a middleweight boxer. I refused. Our PT instructor offered me a crisp one-pound note, with another to follow if I won the bout. I refused. (This, of course, was before Burt Reynolds became a star. My hero at that time was Denis Price.) I went to see the tournament. The middleweight event was a bloodbath. The two opponents stood toe to toe, taking it in turns to pound each other in the face. The canvas was littered with fragments of teeth, scraps of gum, slivers of lip and strands of eyebrow. I reaffirmed my vow to stick to whist. I had only been asked to box because of my agility in the Naafi queues; this reputation dogged me.

I played rugby for the battalion – once. 'Aspel, are you delirious with success?' screeched our captain, as I made a determined burst for the line. 'Oh, you leprous animal!' he continued, as he realised I wasn't carrying a ball.

They asked me to make up the numbers for the hockey team. Dangerous, I said. I'm going on leave tomorrow. No problem, they said – just keep the stick low and your eye on the puck. Which is what I did, and came off the field with a swollen eye and a bleeding nose, with a friction burn across my chin from the bloody puck.

Let's have a look at that list again. Gymnastics: well, I *was* pretty good at that at school – shinning up ropes, running on the spot, dodging medicine-balls. Years later, rehearsing *Crackerjack* in an old gymnasium, I wondered if I could still manage that swift climb up the ropes to the ceiling without using the legs. I found I could. I also found I was constipated for a week afterwards, my stomach muscles unable to take further strain.

When the school Boats Club was re-established after the war, I became a member of the First Eight, rowing at number two (up the sharp end on the right-hand side), and I took part in a memorable Head of the River race. We were led by a brave oarsman whose shorts had split and whose private parts were crushed as his legs closed at the end of each stroke. How we rowed!

When I moved to Wales and found to my relief that there was little or no rowing to be had, I joined a tennis club. Most of the members seemed to serve the ball by giving it a petulant slap in the direction of the net; offended by this 'effeteness', I determined to play powerhouse tennis – aces all the way. I did, indeed, learn to serve strongly. That was all I learned. If anybody returned my service, that was that. I don't think I ever won a game. Except, that is, against my wife. I remember that day well. Back and forth we surged, no quarter asked or given, advantage her, advantage me. Eventually she admitted defeat. Our son was born the next day.

Pole-vaulting – well, that's summed up in a school photograph which unfortunately

I've lost. It's a splendid action shot, and shows me clearing the bar in fine style. I appear to be high in the air, but the effect is marred slightly by some sneaky first-former seen watching from the sidelines. He is looking *down*.

I learned to swim while I was a wartime evacuee. The American troops who were stationed near the village used to throw coins and tinned food into the local reservoir, and we would go in after it. Without this plunder I doubt if we would have survived. I never learned to swim far, or fast. Consistent with my belief that it is better to travel than to arrive, my aim was to perfect my diving technique. Ah, those heart-stopping aerial gymnastics – the swallow dive, the jack-knife, and best of all, the forward-rolling triple somersault with the double-whammy flip; achieved by few, and never by me.

Jokari is a game I can recommend to sportsmen who prefer to go it alone. It is ostensibly a game for two, and consists of a block of wood to which is attached a length of strong elastic with a small rubber ball at the end: you take it in turns to bash this rubber ball with wooden bats. Depending on the strength and angle of the strike, and the state of the ground, the ball will fly back in interesting ways – to your forearm, to your backhand, above your head, but most likely, it will bury itself deep in your groin. The best way to play the game is by yourself. Then you can thrash your imaginary opponent, set up your own world records and work up a satisfactory lather without losing any dignity or wagers.

Snooker, probably the most therapeutic of all games, is another I prefer to do solo. The ideal situation is a deserted games room at 2am at some expensive hotel. The room is heavy with your cigar-smoke, the brandy is at hand, and in your mind's eye The Cincinnati Kid and Minnesota Fats watch you enviously from the shadows.

I lied about the sky-diving. I've never done it, though I have leapt fearfully from military aircraft from a height of one thousand feet on several occasions. This was because I had been posted to an airborne TA battalion and was more worried about being dubbed a 'penguin' than of being dashed to pieces on the rocks below. I completed the course and earned my wings but remained terrified of heights. Anything over eight feet and the backs of the knees start to go.

Cricket. Oh well. It would have been nice to take my score into double figures, just once in my life. I simply do not understand how someone who is supple, keen-eyed, well-coordinated and with lightning reflexes can be a failure at the game. And if *he's* no good, what chance do I stand? Occasionally, by the law of averages, I have sauntered out to the wicket, pleading 'be gentle with me' and then struck the friendly lob to the boundary. Then they say, 'Right, you bastard' and stick me to the sight-screen like a butterfly.

But I have some glorious memories of idyllic afternoons and riotous evenings with the old TV Travellers and the BBC News team (Richard Baker bowling underarm); I have been allowed to tread some hallowed turfs and shake some illustrious hands, and my proudest possession is the sweater that Jim Laker wore when he got his nineteen wickets against some foreigners twenty-odd years ago. It's too big for me, but that's the story of my life. Anyone for Ludo?

BRIAN CLOSE
The Groundsman

THE GROUNDSMAN

I've done most things in cricket in my time, except prepare a wicket, or in other words act as groundsman. With all those years of experience behind me, I would think that this essay is my first and last escapade into this aspect of the game!

The groundsman cannot win, and that wouldn't do for me! If he prepares a wicket with lots of runs in it, he suffers the wrath of the bowlers. If the wicket helps the bowler too much, he has the batsmen moaning. If it is 'just right', the players and their cricket receive the accolades. The wicket is either too flat, too slow, too quick, too green, too bare, too damp – or too something else. He can please some people, some of the time, but never can he please all of them, all of the time.

In the course of my years in cricket (fourteen as captain), in my memory I have only ever reported a wicket once – and that was when the wicket was more like Blackpool sands than the real thing. No, I actually enjoyed a battle on a none-too-good wicket. On flat, easy-paced wickets, any batsman can make runs if he has the patience to stay around and not throw his wicket away foolishly. On less than good wickets, however, it takes ability, technique, application and guts to make runs. When the ball is turning sharply or lifting occasionally, that is when an ice-cool brain, razor-sharp senses and reflexes are needed, to guide the bat into line to smother the dangers. This is when the men are separated from the boys, the occasion that either brings the best out of a batsman or crushes him into submission, the occasion when batsmen can *really* say that they have won a game for their side – when every run counts at least double.

In England we have always favoured uncovered wickets, and I hope we never change that system as long as the game is played. The reason? Well, on good wickets, covered all the time from the elements, the play generally falls into a routine. In these circumstances we see such a lot of stereotyped play, often falling into a defensive pattern by the team in the field – and it takes a good side with an imaginative skipper to raise the cricket to an exciting and dramatic pitch. So few captains are prepared to experiment, to give a few runs away, and keep trying different things in order to make the game go their way. When the wicket is good, the whipping boys are the bowlers. They keep slogging away, putting lots of energy into their job with often little return. Isn't it good for him to turn over in his mind the thought 'the boot may be on your foot now, but just wait until I get you on a lively, rain-affected wicket – I'll make you jump for it then'! Encouraging thoughts for a bowler.

The captains need the co-operation of the groundsman at the beginning of the match in particular. I always tried to establish a rapport with them and create a friendly atmosphere, so that they would inform me of what had been done in preparing the wicket. For example, when the wicket had last been watered – what had happened in previous games – which types of bowlers had taken wickets, and so on. You need answers to all such questions, in order to pick the best team for the match, and to have an idea of what might happen during the game. To be forewarned is to be forearmed, as they say!

Groundsmen are generally sincere, warm-hearted people, who have often played the game in earlier life at some level. They naturally like their work to be appreciated. There is nothing so exhilarating as to play cricket on a beautiful ground, well manicured, freshly cut, and looking like a huge snooker table with a hard brownish strip in the centre.

What constitutes a good wicket? Not necessarily lots of grass – grass is there primarily for the roots to hold and bind the soil – perhaps just a fine layer to protect the surface a little. We've all heard of the need for quick, pacey wickets. However, in my judgement, the main requisite for good, positive cricket is good, even bounce. With decent bounce in the wicket, the bowler feels that if he beats the batsman and gets the edge, he has a chance the ball will carry to his slips or short-legs. Therefore it encourages him to attack, exhibit his skills, and get a few fieldsmen close in, in catching positions. At the same time, from a batsman's point of view, if he is playing well enough and the bad ball comes along, it bounces nicely for him to take advantage and punish it. Thereby you can get a good balance – good bowling rewarded, and plenty of runs at the right tempo. It all helps to create a good game, with skill getting its just reward: and what more do we want than that?

As a parting shot, I'll tell you of the time that the great Yorkshire side of the late fifties and sixties got a telling off by the chairman. As you know, Yorkshire play matches on seven different grounds. Well, we used to turn up at the grounds on the first morning of the match, and on the less famous grounds nearly always found a thick layer of grass on the wicket. A wicket like this often has quite a bit of life in it early on for seam bowlers, but as the moisture dissipated it usually got better and better from a batsman's point of view. It obviously helped much poorer sides than ours to hold out against us, and generally boiled down to a long hard slog for three full days. Even at the end we were not sure we would get a result out of the game.

Well, on one occasion the Yorkshire lads turned up for a match – and if the wicket hadn't been pitched and the markings painted, we wouldn't have known from any other part of the square where the wicket was going to be. It looked as if it hadn't *seen* a mower, and to make matters worse the other county were strong in seam bowling against our strength in swing and spin. After a little persuasion, the groundsman (new to the job) got his mower out and took off a thick layer of grass. Now it looked like a wicket and the result was a Yorkshire win. However, the groundsman complained to the committee, and a few days later the team were hauled over the coals for interference in another's job. As a result, with our fingers burnt we didn't dare ever to interfere again; and that has been my policy ever since.

DONALD
PLEASANCE
Physio

DREAMS OF GREATNESS

When I was twelve, I mounted my bike and cycled from Sheffield to Huddersfield with another boy from my school. The mighty Yorkshire eleven (then fielding six or seven of the England team) were being thrashed by Essex. My friend's uncle was a member of Yorkshire, and he had given us passes to the Huddersfield pavilion. We were too late for the finish. The great Essex bowlers, Farnes and Nichols, had dismissed Yorkshire for a handful of runs in each innings.

Disgruntled Yorkshire cricketers, unused to being beaten, were leaving the pavilion. My friend and I clutched our autograph books shyly. We were not accustomed to being so close to the great. Hedley Verity obliged. Bill Bowes (mop of blond hair, thick glasses) leaned over and signed from an immense height. We approached Sutcliffe. 'Not now!' He walked on briskly. A young man with a long, melancholy face was following him. He signed our books and seemed pleased to be asked. He was unknown to us. The voice of Herbert Sutcliffe snapped from the gate, 'Come on, Len!'. The future captain of England followed like a dog.

Cricket was my opium. In father's goods-yard (he was a station master) day after day and hour after hour I took a twenty-five yard run and hurled the ball at the three stumps chalked up on the goods' shed wall, twenty-two yards away. I was Larwood, I was Voce, sometimes I was Bill Bowes, though I was less than five feet tall. I never hit the stumps. I didn't even make the school third eleven.

I have always fantasised about cricket. Even now, on sleepless nights, I can dismiss the entire Australian eleven for a dozen runs. My friend Robert Shaw (in his life a great cricket fantasist) once came bright-eyed into the dressing room we were sharing. He had dreamed that he was the fastest and most accurate bowler in the world. How could he convince the England selectors?

'Perhaps you could hurl one down the Long Room at Lord's', I said.

'Take this seriously!' said Robert. 'I know it's a fantasy but there *might* be somebody who could do it. How could you convince these people?'

'Well Robert', I said, 'you could creep on to Lord's cricket ground when the England team is at the nets, then choose a place about twenty yards from the bowler's wicket, make a great cry and faint. The players will all gather round you. Someone is certain to drop a cricket ball. You seize the ball, run up the twenty yards and hurl it at the middle stump. They will perceive that you are the fastest and most accurate bowler in the world.'

I was asked to open a charity cricket match and to bowl the first over. Shall I take four wickets, I wondered, or five? I polished the ball lightly on my quite unsuitable grey trousers and started my run from twenty yards away. The first ball was so wide that a gorilla, reaching out and playing a cross-bat shot, could not have reached it. Two no-balls and a long-hop followed. With a slight smile, I handed the ball to the umpire. My face seemed to say, 'I *could* do it, but I'm only here to entertain.'

BRIAN
CLOUGH
The Manager

THE MANAGER'S ROLE

The first thing that I would do as cricket manager would be to put five years on the playing life of my captain. And I'm not joking. It's absolutely staggered me over the years that captains of cricket clubs at every level are saddled with such tremendous responsibility. How they manage to perform on the field I'll never know.

The captain is involved with selecting teams, making sure that everybody turns up to do his job and, above all, he is making major decisions in every single minute of every cricketing day. That's enough to explode any captain's mind, and it is little wonder that some of them fail to produce the goods themselves. I doubt if they have any time left to worry about their own personal performances.

On top of all that, the captains are the men who take the brunt of criticism when things go wrong. You've heard the kind of comments you get from the members' stand . . . 'He should have been off half an hour ago' . . . 'What's he doing opening the batting?' . . . I could go on, but like me, you've heard it all before.

And at the end of the day when you've won or lost, you've still got to face committees. If it's your misfortune to be involved with some of the officials that I've met in football and cricket, good luck to you because you'll need it. Having to sort things out with some of the men I've come across in sport is enough to send any captain to the brink of despair. And beyond it on occasions.

So what would a manager do? He'd provide a buffer for a start between the officials and the captain and players, and rule out some of the work that secretaries have done in cricket.

It is mind-boggling when you consider the responsibilities that secretaries have had from a cricketing point of view. Their job is administration – not running cricket teams.

Having sorted that lot out – and I probably wouldn't fall far short of revolutionising the whole game – I'd get cracking with the players. Listening to some of them in dressing rooms and pavilions, I've never heard so many defeatists in my life. Some of them actually talk themselves out before they've got their pads on!

Players have got to be built up, whether they are cricketers, footballers or anyone else. They have to believe they are capable of doing well, otherwise they may as well sit in the bar all day. It's an attitude of mind more than anything else, and I'm delighted that Yorkshire have now got a man in Raymond Illingworth who is capable of sorting out all the problems that a manager is paid to do.

I am sure that his appointment will be followed by many more. If I ever get lost for a job in football, I might be on the market myself . . .

MIKE
BREARLEY
Substitute

SUBSTITUTES

A substitute has a thankless task. On tour, he is reminded before each Test: 'You are only a stomach upset away from playing.' But actually poisoning his rival seems to be a bit much. He does not play, and the five days pass slowly. It is hard to feel part of the team that celebrates, or drowns its sorrows, at the end of the match. My main experience of the role was on the tour of South Africa in 1964–65. David Brown and I were reduced to playing personal 'Tests' in the nets. At other times, we took wet clothing to be dried in the sun, and catered to the needs of the players in the dressing-room and at drinks intervals. Bob Barber and I were interrupted during a chess-game by his innings at Johannesburg. When I took his dry gloves on to the field, he greeted me with the words 'Pawn to QB3'. I was not allowed to take the chess-board out with me at drinks.

The general consensus of more recent substitutes is that the fussiest player is my old friend Alan Knott. 'The Flea' always wants something they do not have: a dry handkerchief to wipe his face, or a wet one to cool his neck; or sticky tape to keep his shirt-cuffs down below the tops of his wicket-keeping gloves. His drink requirement was predictable, though: he would ask for a Coke, then shake it and squirt out the fizz.

Another substitute role is that of runner. When a batsman is seen to be limping at the wicket, I have noticed that those who are already out tend to disapppear into the showers or round the back of the pavilion. We sent Derek Randall in as runner for Bob Taylor at Perth; the instructions were that all the calling should be left to the other batsman, who was, I think, Geoff Miller. Within minutes the voices of all three could be heard debating a run, and the loudest of the three was Randall's. Richard Austin was called upon to run for Clive Lloyd in the last of the World Series one-day finals at Melbourne; he thought that he had to run from square-leg (where he stood when Lloyd was the striker) to the stumps at the bowler's end, and then back along the same diagonal and rather longer route, until Greg Chappell told him that he could run parallel to the pitch. Having a runner is often a recipe for chaos: the injured batsman forgets the pain and hares off down the wicket with his puzzled runner trying to keep up with him. If there is no famous photograph of all three racing for the same crease with bats stretched out in front of them and heads grimly down, then there ought to be.

Substitutes carry messages to and from the battle-front, like that helpful instruction from a desperate captain, 'Score at eight an over but don't take risks'. Or, more constructively, the message may be to look out for fielders changing their positions as the bowler runs into bowl, or to complain about the opposition's substitute fielding in a specialist catching position. Messages come the other way, too, as when, at Perth, Clive Radley brought back Ian Botham's suggestion that 'someone should get "Boycs" a fishing-net', after he had dropped two 'skiers' off Botham in ten minutes.

For Test matches, England require two substitutes to be on hand when we field, and one to cater to the batsmen's needs when we are batting. John Lever and Phil Edmonds, being excellent fielders, had the former task for four Tests in Australia in 1978–79. When we batted first, they would watch for the first hour or so, then leave the ground for the beach. But they had scarcely settled down to the day's serious sunbathing when their transistor told them of another first-innings batting collapse. It's a hard life. But of course it *is* a hard life, and one that has an important effect for good or bad on team spirit over a tour or a county season.

In club cricket, substitutes are rare if not unheard of, except for the embarrassing situation that occurs when no one has remembered to tell old Alf that he has been dropped for this week's match, and twelve have turned up. The youngster who always packs his boots in the tremulous hope of a game is likely to be less cynical about the position of reserve than the professional, who because of some chance concomitance of talent finds himself left out match after match. One die-hard Yorkshire supporter for years carried his gear to Yorkshire matches, dreaming of the occasion when a player would fail to appear, and he, as the only Yorkshire-born male spectator between the ages of fifteen and sixty-five, would get a game for the county. He did not, as it happened, step on to the field, but his boots did. Richard Hutton's sole fell off at Portsmouth, and the boots, at least, made their debut as substitutes.

NEIL
DURDEN-SMITH
The Kitty

THE KITTY

'Kitty', says *The Concise Oxford Dictionary* – though being ordered as well as concise, it does not start there. 'Kittul' precedes; 'kiwi' follows. 'Pool in some card games; joint fund (How much is there left in the kitty?); (bowls) [jack 19th C; origin unknown]'. It is the second meaning that concerns the cricketer. How much indeed? And how many times is the question bounced off empty beer mugs in the bar?

The square brackets at the end of the definition contain significance too. Origin unknown? Perhaps, but the nineteenth century. That is more definite than it need be – definite but not surprising. For was it not in the second half of last century that the public schools and their produce were drawing up the rules of team games and drumming in the virtues of team spirit? And is not a joint fund the natural extension of the code to life after school, and life after a match?

The kitty insists that everyone should contribute equally, which circumstances on the field have shown can never be the case. The kitty is the outward and visible sign of the enduring spirit of the game: it invites the man who conceded a penalty to be on a par with another who scored a hat-trick. It equates prop with three-quarter, prodigal with cheeseparer. It enables the tight fist and the open hand to stand elbow to elbow. It reminds the non-bowler that he is as important as the wicket-taker, the run-machine that he is no more so than the rabbit. It entitles the duffer of deckchair and deep Third Man to drink man to man with the demons of bat and ball. It lifts and lowers till all are level. It is a subscription to camaraderie.

It might be thought that the kitty principle is a recipe for harmony, an example to be applied with advantage to life at large. Sportsmen, though, know that practice seldom follows the simple trace of theory. Complications beyond the bounds of reasonable contemplation crop up in the collection of eleven dues from eleven men until the operation becomes a nightmare of logistics. Players drop out on the morning of a match for fear that the captain's finger will point at them for the task. Wrists which can caress the ball through the covers may be slashed. Heads which rise high in the line-out are stuck in gas ovens. Accountants come tight-lipped with pen and paper, top men in the City arrive ashen, with calculators. And even then the thing never adds up. The sum is not eleven times the toll. So why the fuss and why the trembling? The wise captain knows his men or may even collect the kitty himself.

On the face of it, the problems are fewer in cricket than in rugby. The niggard from the woodpile of a rugby scrum can nip off under cover of the plunge-bath's steam. There is time, though, for cricket's tax collector to drift with innocent *bonhomie* among the team, strolling the boundary with one, nobbling another at tea, catching a third with his trousers down but not without money in his pockets. The opportunities are ample, but so many are scorned for Parkinson (not the one who puts Boycott on the box) had a law, and it does not become the game to count pounds and pence during play. The reckoning then is in runs and wickets.

So the duty is deferred, the game becomes more or less diverting in its close, and suddenly it is too late. The gates are wide open for the skinflints' escape. The thriftless have scattered. The labour is Herculean. A few are in the bar already, buying a round regardless, a jug and then another for the opposition. Husbands are sharing the sunset with wives and gin-and-tonic. Father is down at the nets, doing duty with son. The belles have claimed their blades. Scrooge is under the shower, won't be a moment . . . gone. Another pops home to change, will be back, is not. This one only has a fiver; last week it was a tenner. The vicar has beamed off to Evensong, might be able to raise it later – depends on the congregation.

And so it goes on. 'That makes five; six if I count myself, seven So-and-so; eight . . .'

'How much is there left in the kitty?', the cry rings out again.

The collector knows he has failed, curses his lot, condemns the shirkers, hates himself for his incompetence, his gullibility. It is the same, week after week, and the spending compounds the misery of collection, the inequality.

The munificent dig again, another fifty pence, unquestioning on the waves of heartiness. Stalwarts follow suit, wondering what happened to the first contribution, recognising poor value for money, respecting obligation. Others make excuses, grudging as they grudged each run scored off their bowling; they have a dinner waiting – just remembered – and a wife too, most likely. (Wives are a good excuse.) The mean do not stop to explain. They will have worked out their money's worth like their average, consumed it with peculiar satisfaction and been off at the first hint of a second levy. The car engine has not actually been running; that would be wasteful. But bat and bag are stowed ready for a quick getaway. The kitty-master spots him go, and coughs up himself.

And so it goes on, in circles of decreasing size and fairness until, when all is said and done and most of it too late, it is a wonder there is any team spirit left at all. But then cricket is only an image of that larger life; and for every man who is first to the pub to order the opening round, there is another with short arms and long pockets ready to leave before the last, which is his.

The true masters, of course, take the kitty by the whiskers, sort the whole thing out with press-gang dispatch and arrange that something is left at the end. They will not be out of pocket. The majority, though, pay dearly for the chore, forfeiting runs in distraction and forking out more than their share later. When *The Concise Oxford Dictionary* goes into its next edition, revision is due: 'Kitty . . . joint fund (usually empty); *crick.fig.* monument to injustice.'

JUDITH
CHALMERS

Tea Lady

TEA LADIES

After cricket, no ceremony in the English canon is conducted with quite the reverence of tea; and after tea, cricket. Nothing then is more appropriate to the summer game than the tea interval which interrupts it. It is as important as the whiteness of flannels, the taking of guard, the squareness of legs, the signal of fours: while those who direct it are as important as the umpires.

Cricket's tea ladies are as no other purveyors of the post-meridian position. Put one in an identification parade with the queens of canteen, café and country house, and the cricketer will pick her out unerringly, not by the earrings in red and yellow nor, in pouring, by the prominent left elbow. Cricket's tea ladies conform to no style. The tale is told in their eyes, soft with spaniel devotion for those whose own devotion is so obsessive with the manners of the game that they may forget the simple 'thank-yous' of civility. Those eyes convey the ultimate in female understanding, be it at Lord's or in the lowly cattle shed which serves as the headquarters of the village team.

These ladies may not know a stump from a short leg. They may never see a ball bowled, nor care to; such keenness might lead to the scorer's duty. They may not know the score, or, if they do, its meaning, and whether it is good or bad. They may not know, but they understand. They have learned to play themselves in in the small talk which accompanies their service, to shun the hook-shots of commitment – the 'well done' or 'oh dear' – and settle instead for gentle strokes of caution – the 'oh yes' and 'really?'. They recognise the symptoms of apoplectic potential and avoid the question which may light its fuse. They are indeed computers of cricket sympathy, sensing when to speak or smile and where to stop, processing each remark and following it with intuitive intelligence.

Margie Townsend has been at Lord's for twenty-eight years dispensing tea and tact and good spirits (there is a licence too at the long counter in the Pavilion, which is her beat for the Members' refreshment). She went there when her sons grew up and were off her hands. They were sporting mad; Gary played soccer for Millwall. She was already graduating in the arts which are greater even than the acts – the arts of unspoken philosophy which can save a man from despair who has missed a sitter in a cup tie.

Not a Member would disagree. If England come in at 130 for 8 the world will not quite be at an end in the Members' tea-room. She will be ready for the mood, the faces longer than the Long Room; and the teeth will not gnash on doughnuts alone. Her white head, cocked like that of a sparrow on the *qui vive*, she will listen if that is right, or talk if that is better, her eye quizzically clear, puzzling, and penetrating to a point of light beyond darkness. And the Members go back for the final session, their MCC ties intact. Life is still just worth living.

Mrs Townsend would make a first-class umpire if she knew an off-break, but her hours are longer without interval than the hours of play. It is the same in the banqueting rooms, where a lady known as 'Tutts' commands a squad of waitresses in the black uniform of soccer referees, except that the referees do not wear white sporrans for aprons. Tutts might be Colin Milburn's mother if her surname was not Coutts. Her team comes from an agency, but the same ones return year after year. Many are from Ireland where they know less than ever of cricket – but the eyes have a legendary smile.

This is the place for non-members, but they have their regulars – the huddled figures in the background of the first photographs in April, who will be the sad faces of September's parting too. There may be twenty of them a day for lunch and tea, and Tutts is their Mother Superior. There was one elderly raincoat who was always grousing and the waitresses, try as they would, could do nothing to humour him. One day he was particularly awkward, wailing on about lack of salmon as if enough woe might make it appear on the menu. Tutts, keeping the secret to herself, sent over to the Pavilion, where salmon was on. The raincoat lit up like the plastic mac of a traffic cop. Now he eats out of the waitresses' hands – and the china isn't bad.

Such ladies as these are professionals. The great majority, though, are amateurs – the distaff side, present and potential, of cricket's gentlemen, consists of a great body of wives and girlfriends who may be corralled under the banner 'Sandwich Makers'. It is estimated that there are fifty thousand cricket clubs in Britain. If each plays on average once a weekend, there are half a million matches a summer. If each player's ration is one sandwich per game, cricket consumes twenty-two million slices of cut loaf before the spectators have had a bite. The loaves could pave a hundred acres.

Sandwiches are but the beginning of a tea lady's toil, the bread and butter of devotion, though they have been the end too of many a budding romance. Next come the cakes and extras, what a mean Australian, charging for service, would itemise as 'sundries'. Dedication knows no greater expression than home-made jam and scones. Many run no further than the Swiss roll and assorted biscuits. Fruit-cake is an overthrow, except in odd clubs where the ladies are on a rota of rivalry. Then a kind of on-going village fête cake competition is held, whose judges, deep in the state of the game, no more know the rôle than a roll. 'Very nice, dear, thank you' and back to that creamy cover drive. It is probably as well for harmony's sake. They understand.

The tea itself, the liquid centre of the twenty minutes, is the least of the ladies' worries. This is no occasion for the fine arts of the Orient. There will probably be two tin teapots, dented as an old campaigner's box, and an urn and, assuming the right size was bought for a twenty-two man thirst plus umpires and scorers, there is no risk of cricket's greatest catastrophe: a run-out. The only sin is not to be ready. Delicate declarations can founder on delay, batsmen lose their eye in a queue, bowlers their rhythm in a gulp. The ladies usually get it right.

But then any old tea lady can manage that – and young ones too. (There is no age limit.) These are mere routines. Cricket's tea ladies have a sixth sense which transforms the mechanics of the operation to the spiritual level of things before and after.

For two hours swords have been drawn, hits scored; shortly they will be drawn again, for revenge or further advantage. Who then but the English would sit the contestants down between times to lick wounds with one another and chocolate fingers? And who else would think of having their ladies and loved ones in charge? It is crazy but it works, and it works because these paragons read between the lines of blood and sweat and ritual conversation, and respect that the runs and wickets are a code whose key they were never meant to have.

Some of course do know what's what and score points for provocation of enemy rotters – 'that was a good knock, Tom', knowing full well that Tom has snicked and carved a flunky forty off the fuming bowler who is next in line with cup and saucer. But mostly the ladies play safe, keeping an end up with nod and knowing look, fearing for the temper of the evening if a word is spoken out of turn. For who are they to be sure that 4 for 27 is good, if it might have been 5 for 18? Congratulation is dangerous, consolation no safer.

A run-of-the-mill mistress of the pot would put her high heel through the mysteries in no time. But cricket's tea ladies know the ground and have learned to tread carefully through the minefield of ducks, dropped catches and outrageous lbws. It will all come out in the wash of the ensuing week and that, in all probability, is their next act of devotion. They are the last people in the world to march in protest but cricketers should never count on it. After all, they have their sandwich-boards.

RACHAEL
HEYHOE-FLINT
Cricket Widow

THE CRICKET WIDOW

I'm not sure whether I should be classed as a cricket widow, or whether my husband, Derrick, should be dubbed a cricket widower. The point is that we both play cricket practically every weekend throughout the summer – booking out on Saturday morning and then meeting again either on Sunday evening or Monday morning. At least that way it cuts down on the potential number of arguments we are likely to have!

Derrick used to play for Warwickshire back in the dark ages (and that's not referring to the influx of overseas players either). He played at the time when only two stumps were used, which made it very difficult to ask the umpire for a guard of 'centre'.

Accordingly we became engaged at the end of one cricket season and married within three months, so that we didn't interfere with any overseas tours.

At the beginning of my husband's first season after we were married (that's cricket season, I mean, not any other season) I decided I would get Derrick's cricket gear ready for his first match. I opened his cricket bag on Friday, 21 April 1972 – which was my first mistake, because it had remained zippered-up since Sunday, 19 September 1971! His socks leaped out at me – I think they were what you call living socks – but I wasn't quite sure what to feed them on. I now know what Pandora felt like when she opened her box. (Although I never knew she wore one.) Down at the bottom of the bag were some books of raffle tickets from Derrick's club, all unsold, and they should have been returned by June 1970. A crumpled sheet of newspaper was wedged down the back of the bag, and it actually made very interesting reading. For instance, did you know when the QE II was launched? The faded newspaper revealed all about the launch the previous day . . . 20 September 1967!

It really is very useful for a woman cricketer like me to have a husband who understands my love for the game (of cricket!). He understands why he has to have salad every Saturday for lunch during the summer because I am invariably away cricketing or I am in such a rush to get off to my own cricket, that cooking is definitely out. Mind you, cooking is definitely out as far as I'm concerned anyway, summer or winter. I've never really had much time to practise. But when my husband did see my first effort at making a cake, he remarked that it looked lovely, but who on earth helped me to lift it out of the oven . . . such a playful sense of humour!

There again, once my husband gets off to his cricket his troubles are over, but mine are only just beginning! If, for example, I have a home club match for Wolverhampton Ladies and we are fielding first, as part of my captain's tactics I have to remember that my most important decision at 16.00 hours precisely, is to call out to the girls waiting to come into bat, up in the pavilion – 'Please could you switch the tea urn on'.

You see we, unfortunately, just don't have our menfolk making the teas for us – that really would be women's lib gone berserk. We solve our tea-making problem by each player bringing 'tea for two'; the trouble is that we never liaise with one another, and some weeks we all bring fish paste sandwiches or another time we all bring Swiss rolls. (Anyone want to buy two gross of Swiss rolls, untouched by human foot?)

When my son, Benjamin, was in his babyhood (he is now four and a half) I obviously took him along with me to cricket matches, but you can imagine the paraphernalia I had to load into the car. As well as my cricket gear I crammed in one potty for the use of, sunshade (collapsible), playpen (collapsible), carrycot (collapsible), carrycot wheels (collapsible) and labrador (non-collapsible until she reached the age of sixteen, and then her back legs did go a bit). This load was apart from all my son's toys, rattles, disposable nappies and jars of Gerbers food, which the dog quite enjoyed one day when my back was turned.

As Benjamin grew up into a well balanced lad (he even laughs when I mention the name Geoff Boycott, and you have to be well balanced to do that!), he began to understand the game of cricket except that he found the word 'pavilion' very difficult. So it has now been re-named the palivion, which I think sounds much nicer. We even had to keep cricket in mind when choosing Benjamin's name. His paternal grandfather was Benjamin Flint, who used to play cricket for Nottinghamshire, so that was easy. Then we realised that if he wasn't given any other name his cricket bag, in the future, would be initialled 'B.F.'. Then we thought that many of England's best cricketers had three initials – D.C.S. Compton, R.W.V. Robins, P.B.H. May, A.P.E. Knott and T.C.C. Board. (Who?) So then we inserted the name Giles, because we thought he looked rather like a cartoon character, and the Heyhoe for the sake of his maternal grandfather – who was so forward thinking as to teach me cricket from the age of batolescence.

Perhaps one day B.G.H. Flint might have his name in highlights, but I haven't yet taught him not to smile and look pleased when I return to the pavilion far more quickly than either he anticipated or I hoped. I loved the day he said in a very loud, chuckling voice in front of a large crowd, when I had been dismissed third ball, 'You didn't get many runs did you Mummy'. I had to call on all my Oscar-winning acting ability to squeeze a smile out of my fury for my little darling. Then I dragged him (gently) into the dressing room and made him read *Wisden* from front to back cover before he came out into the sunshine again.

Life in our house seems to revolve round cricket, especially at Test match time; we have to have a television in the kitchen so that we don't miss a ball bowled when I am in there pretending to be domestic, or when my husband is eating his twenty-eighth salad of the summer.

In order not to upset our sunbathing activities, we have a huge extension-lead so that we can have one television going out on the lawn. This is always accompanied by the transistor, so that we can listen to ball-by-ball commentary on Radio Three when the dog decides to sit in front of the television screen. (She likes the shade which we have constructed round the set, so that we can see some faint sort of a picture.) Our lunchtime runs from 1.30 to 2.10 and my afternoon tea with Benjamin from 4.20 to 4.40 – and no attempt at cooking supper or putting little B. to bed is made before 6.35 and the close of play summary.

Yet there are distinct advantages in being wedded to a cricketer; you never run out of ideas of what to give for presents at Christmas or birthday time. I give Derrick my old bat and he gives me his old gloves! But nowadays there are even more cricket products to widen your range of anniversary gifts – useful things such as thigh pads, crash helmets, gum shields, coconut shells and breast plates of righteousness.

It also has the advantage, being married to a cricketer, that you can both go away together on a cricket tour and *both* enjoy yourselves – rather than one going away and leaving the other full of doubt, misery (or perhaps even untold happiness) at home.

I took a team of international women cricketers to Canada in the summer of 1977; we were guests of the Toronto Men's Cricket Club to help celebrate their one hundred and fiftieth anniversary. Derrick, my step-daughter, Rowan, and Benjamin came along too, and we made a super family holiday out of the trip. The only one upsetting part of the tour was when Derrick, guesting for the Canada/UK Forty Club XI against us, walked out to bat resplendent in his Warwickshire sweater (and trousers of course!). I was meanwhile telling the girls that he was quite useful and very strong on the leg side (and on the cricket field as well). So imagine my mortification, and even more so Derrick's, when he was clean bowled first ball – just as he was getting settled as well! I think there and then he might have packed up and gone home (except we were all on a group ticket). In fact what materialised was that because I scored more than Derrick in that match, I ended up buying *him* a drink!

To be serious for just one moment though (so you thought I had been for the last fifteen hundred words, eh?) it is fantastic to have a husband who understands me. It certainly isn't the case in our household that I say 'my husband doesn't understand me'. When I was playing and captaining England in 1976 against Australia at The Oval in the the third and final Test, we as a team were in dire straits and in danger of losing a twenty-five year unbeaten Test record. I batted in our second innings on the penultimate day for two and a half hours to the close, and was given valuable support by the other players. If we were to avoid defeat, I knew we would have to produce a superhuman effort on the final day to avoid an innings defeat. I was exhausted at the end of the third day so I rang Derrick at home in Wolverhampton from our London hotel (no expenses spared – transfer charge!) and said I would have to produce all sorts of miracles on the last day to survive. Without hesitation (because he was paying for the call) Derrick said he would come to London next morning (a) to support me and (b) to drive me home.

I managed to survive the morning session with magnificent assistance from the other players in our side. By lunch-time I was on my knees, but knew I had to battle on if I could for two more sessions – four hours batting in all. Part way through the afternoon session I saw Derrick arrive and take his seat just by the gangway in front of the pavilion. It gave me tremendous heart to know that he had arrived, and psychologically it helped me enormously. Suffice it to say, we survived, and I (immodestly) was dismissed off the last ball of the day, caught out going for a six to celebrate survival – with my score on 179.

As I dragged myself up the pavilion steps, Derrick greeted me at the top, with a hug and a smacker – and a sip of beer – well, there's no end to his generosity. But then he bought champagne for the team and it made me realise how smashing it is to be married to a cricket widower and how 'smashinger' it is to be a cricket widow!

TIM
RICE
The Captain

CLOSE OF PLAY: STUMPS

Well that's it. No more sparkling essays or wonderful pictures for you to savour, gentle reader, unless of course you are one of those individuals who always nips to the back of any book first to see who did it. I can reveal now that it was Colonel Mustard with the grease gun in the billiard room. But don't let the fact that you now know who the murderer is stop you from buying this book, if you haven't already done so. The Lord's Taverners need every penny in royalties that this volume can muster, and on behalf of the talented team who have put the whole shooting match together, may I thank everyone who has decided, or who is about to decide, to add this tome to their library.

As the light fails and as the last spectators drift away from the green, my thoughts turn from the game just played, from the book just completed, to the idea of a musical about cricket. American box office potential may not be great but what about Sydney and Bombay, not to mention the West End? First draft plot: Two village teams get together to fix the breaking of A.E.J. Collins long-standing record individual score of 628 not out for financial gain. It's a three-day game, played on three consecutive Saturdays and the twenty-two cads arrange things so that one man is about 570 not out at the end of the second Saturday. They then spend the next week setting up film rights, television coverage, and selling exclusive stories to the Sunday papers, as the record seems certain to fall on the third match day. But – shortly before the crucial Saturday, the two teams fall out. The fielding side resent the attention focused on the side that contains the wonder batsman, and are determined to get him out before he scores the final few runs. Tension mounts . . . end of Act One. Please excuse me, I must call Andrew Lloyd Webber.